AID AND THE HELP

T0311320

GLOBALIZATION IN EVERYDAY LIFE

Aid and the Help

*International Development and
the Transnational Extraction of Care*

DINAH HANNAFORD

STANFORD UNIVERSITY PRESS
Stanford, California

Stanford University Press
Stanford, California

Printed in the United States of America on
acid-free, archival-quality paper

ISBN 9781503634602 (cloth)
ISBN 9781503635500 (paper)
ISBN 9781503635517 (ebook)

Library of Congress Control Number: 2022946955

Library of Congress Cataloging-in-Publication
Data available upon request.

Cover design: Susan Zucker
Cover photograph: Ricci Shryock
Typeset by Elliott Beard in Minion Pro 10/14.4

For Maimouna Ciss, with love

Contents

Acknowledgments

I want to thank all the aid workers and domestic workers who spoke to me for this project. They did not owe me their time nor their indulgence as I pestered them with questions about their private lives and their work, and I don't take their generosity for granted. In Senegal, I depended on the kindness of strangers who housed me, as well as the hospitality and deep networks of many friends and loved ones. I will not name the former, as many of them feature in the accounts in this book, but among the latter I offer sincere appreciation to the Niang family, the Dieme family, Ramatoulaye Ndao, Victoria Fletcher, Karen Cobos Latham, Megan Willis, Ricci Shryock, Seynabou "Bebe" Seck, and the late great Gary Engelberg.

This project was supported by the Alexander von Humboldt Foundation, through a postdoctoral research fellowship in 2017–2018. I was hosted by the warm and welcoming Helma Lutz and the Faculty of Social Sciences at Goethe University in Frankfurt, Germany, and enjoyed the intellectual fellowship of Saara Pellander and Greta Wagner. Thanks to Daniel Mains, Paolo Gaibazzi, Abdoulaye Sounaye, and Julian Tedasse at the Leibniz-Zentrum Moderner

Orient (ZMO) in Berlin for including me in their workshop that fall, and to Isabel Pumar, Bekki Smith, Jose Maldonado, Laliv Melamed, Yossi Capua, the staff of K.I.D.S., and the magical Sophie Nowak, all of whom were crucial to the success and productivity of that fellowship year.

At Texas A&M University, Robert Shandley, Carmela Garritano, Stefanie Harris, Portia Owusu, and Maddalena Cerrato provided feedback, resources, and encouragement, and Jocelyn Frelier, Allegra Midgette, Chaitanya Lakkimsetti, and Vanita Reddy created enriching and generative programming. The Ray A. Rothrock '77 Fellowship, the Scowcroft Institute, and the College of Liberal Arts funded parts of my fieldwork as well as other research expenses. The Glasscock Center at Texas A&M University provided not only financial support but opportunities to workshop early parts of this manuscript. I was fortunate to direct a Glasscock Undergraduate Summer Scholars program while completing the book, and my exchanges with superb undergraduate students Jose' Solis and Myranda Campanella helped me clarify my thinking on numerous aspects of development studies.

Opportunities to present pieces of the project to the African Studies Centers at both Boston University and the University of Florida were especially helpful, and I thank Joanna Davidson and Abdoulaye Kane for organizing those talks. Discussions with Ellen Foley, Erik Vickstrom, Caroline Faria, Julie Kleinman, Abena Osseo-Assare, and Joanna Davidson shaped this project in myriad ways, and their interest in the topic gave me tremendous encouragement. Sydney Silverstein's keen eye and generous feedback were invaluable. I offer thanks to Marcela Maxfield, Sunna Juhn, Cindy Lim, and the editorial and production staff at Stanford University Press. Special appreciation goes to Rhacel Parreñas for her early support of the project and my work, as well as to her and Hung Cam Thai for their inclusion of this book in this series.

Working on this project through the onset of the COVID-19 pandemic brought the labor of care into relief in unexpected ways.

This pandemic has laid bare how precarious the balance of work and caring labor is for professional women in most of the world. In the US particularly, where bars and shopping malls were reopened long before schools were, where nursing homes became dangerous places for the elderly, necessitating home care arrangements by relatives, and where workplaces demanded continued productivity "in these challenging times," with the assumption that working parents (read: working moms) would somehow pick up the slack of demanding and under-stimulated children while cleaning up after and catering to a family who is always home, the appeal of outsourcing the burden of domestic maintenance was never more palpable and added much-needed nuance to my understanding of my interlocutors' choices. I was able to move this project forward amid lockdowns, family health crises, and school closures only with the help of Kira Deshler, Marta Zarzycka, William Verheul, Rachel Hannaford, Justin Lerer, and Stephen Hannaford, as well as the miraculous Facetime babysitting services of Janie and Eric Rosenthal.

I feel fortunate to have been raised by Marion Faber, who modeled a work-family balance that took pleasure in each, aimed for perfection in neither, and yet somehow ended up achieving excellence in both. Finally, I count myself tremendously lucky to have an extremely capable domestic partner for whom full participation in parenting, housekeeping, cooking, and other forms of care is instinctive. Adam, nothing functions without you. Charlotte and I are blessed that you put up with our mess.

AID AND THE HELP

INTRODUCTION
AID WORK AND THE EXTRACTION OF CARE

We are leaving Senegal and wish we could take our amazing, sweet and reliable nanny Marietou.[1] She just radiates joy and genuinely enjoys working with babies and kids. She is creative in inventing games and activities, is very patient and great at making my son giggle and roll over with laughter. Marietou has worked with us for a year, taking excellent care of our baby boy since he was 4 months old. Before us, she worked with an American family for 4 years and did US embassy courses on hygiene, safety, etc. Before that, she was employed by a Dutch family for 7 years. Marietou is so sweet, smart, and trustworthy that I have not once worried when I had to leave my baby with her and go to the office. Not once! She goes on and organizes playdates, goes out to the market, cleans while baby naps, and cooks upon request and can stay occasional nights for babysitting. She makes our lives so much easier without us really noticing.

This ad, posted by an international aid worker in a newsletter for people looking to hire domestic workers in Dakar, Senegal, is typical of the kinds of classifieds that expat development workers consult upon arrival to Dakar and post upon their departure. In my years in and alongside the development industry in Senegal, I rarely met an international aid worker who did not employ domestic workers—at the very least a maid or a guard but often a nanny, a cook, a driver, or a gardener as well. In this regard, development workers are no different from expats in Africa who work in the mining industry, in business and telecommunications, or in diplomatic roles.

Hiring domestic workers is a routine part of the expat development lifestyle, not just in Senegal, where my research takes place, but in nearly all locations in which development workers are posted abroad. Expat development workers I knew in Dakar compared experiences hiring nannies in Thailand and Ethiopia, told stories of their guards in Tanzania and their maids in Myanmar. Though nearly every expat aid worker in the developing world has local people working within the intimate sphere of their homes, these relationships are rarely if ever discussed in analyses of the development paradigm and its praxis. Even the studies that focus explicitly on the lived experience of development work rarely ever mention this arrangement or the dynamics surrounding it.[2] Within the context of the notable "parochial cosmopolitanism" (Rajak and Stirrat 2011) of aid workers, who live only a few years in any one location and often spend that time in a "bubble," which Raymond Apthorpe (2005) called "Aidland" to describe how "aid workers inhabit a separate world with its own time, space, and economics," it is remarkable that such reliable and intimate associations with local people could go ignored. Remarkable, but also consistent with how domestic labor itself has been largely invisible to states and policy analysts.[3]

This book addresses this lacuna in studies of international development through an ethnographic analysis of the intersection of development work and domestic work. The relationship between aid workers and their domestic employees, the connection between development work and domestic work, is an apt prism for studying essential realities about the racial, gendered, and classed aspects of the development industry. Examining aid workers as employers of domestic labor provides an opportunity to reach a deeper understanding about the function of development as an orienting framework in our contemporary world, as well as a means to consider the role of aid workers as postcolonial subjects in Africa.

Arlie Hochschild has used the metaphor of extraction in her writing about the global care chain, drawing a parallel between the imperialist extraction of resources like gold and rubber and the current migration of care workers from the developing world to the West. She refers to love as "the new gold" and describes it as being fetishized, in Marx's sense of the term, in that "we unwittingly separate the love between nanny and child from the global capitalist order of love to which it very much belongs" (2003, 26). Spotlighting the outsourcing of reproductive labor—the extraction of care that occurs so regularly in the practice of international development work, the rewards it brings for expats, and the sacrifices and ambivalent opportunities it entails on the part of domestic workers—is an invitation to identify the other multiple ways that the ostensibly "giving" industry of development can be an extractive industry as well.

Following Hannah Appel's recent call to "shift our critical understanding of capitalism from one in which 'markets' merely deepen or respond to postcolonial inequality, to one in which markets are *made* by that inequality" (2019, 2; italics in the original), I align with critical perspectives of the development industry that see it not as an industry that resulted from postcolonial inequity but one that is sustained by and sustains postcolonial inequity. This book is a contribution to efforts to render this critique more tangible and visible.

DAKAR AND THE EXPAT EXPERIENCE

Dakar, Senegal's capital city, is a peninsula on the country's western coast (map 1). A city of about 3 million inhabitants and growing, it comprises nearly a quarter of the country's population. The city's downtown, called le Plateau, was modeled after a French city—with wide boulevards, white buildings, and a central green mall—and has

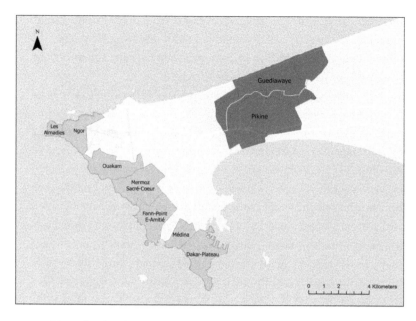

MAP 1. Map of Dakar by Francis Russell.

a distinctly cosmopolitan flare.[4] Its large port made it one of the most important cities in French West Africa, a diverse crossroads for Africans, Arabs, and Europeans, and a center of colonial Afropolitanism (M'baye 2019).[5]

So much of colonial worldmaking took place in African cities, which were the center of the social, economic, and political projects of imperialism, the *lieux colonials* (Coquery-Vidrovitch 1993), and Dakar was no exception. Contemporary Dakar is profoundly shaped by its colonial history in ways that have direct implications for contemporary expatriate life. Like other French West African colonies, Senegal was not considered a "white settler colony." The tropical climate and accompanying maladies like yellow fever, as well as the minimal profitability of the groundnut crop, Senegal's chief export, meant that there was a great deal of turnover of colonial staff. Rather than passing down land for generations as in other colonial settings in Africa, in Senegal Europeans remained expatriates rather than settlers, with regular leave and plans to return definitively to the metropole after completing their work (Cruise O'Brien 1972,17; Mercier 1955, 135). The administration was chronically underfunded and understaffed (Bigon 2016, 8), and a lack of abundant resources meant that European zones of cities like Dakar were prioritized for investing in infrastructure and amenities, thus "the first streets to be paved, lined with trees, lit, properly drained and regulated as *ronds-points* were therefore those of the white residential quarters" (82).

These areas of European residence in the colonial period continue to be the zones where Western expats reside in contemporary Dakar, including the downtown plateau and the coastal neighborhoods of Les Almadies, Ngor, and Mermoz.[6] Though elite Senegalese now also share these zones, which were strictly segregated in the colonial period, they remain characterized by economic exclusivity and thus by a prevalence of expats and businesses that cater to expats.

Though not a settler community, Dakar's place as the eventual center for French colonial administration and industry, and from 1902 to 1960 as the capital of the French West Africa Federation (AOF), meant that the city has long had a strong presence of transitory Europeans and other foreigners.[7] In the last decades before Senegal achieved independence in 1960, it was estimated that more than half the French population living in the whole of West Africa was in Senegal, and the majority of them resided in Dakar (Mercier 1955, 132). It is no less an international metropolis now and still counts a much higher presence of Western residents than other cities in the region (Bigon 2016, 179). The city continues growing and expanding steadily and haphazardly thanks to rampant urbanization, international investment, and large infrastructural projects from a range of global partners.[8]

One of the key industries that continues to bring Westerners to Dakar is international development. Nearly all the well-known global aid agencies have a major presence in Dakar, and the city is home to many regional headquarters for these agencies as well due to its political stability and relatively good infrastructure. Smaller local and grassroots organizations also cluster in Dakar, contracting with the larger agencies or creating their own agendas and fundraising structures. Close to five hundred non-governmental organizations are registered as operating in Senegal, according to the Ministry of Community Development, Social and Territorial Equity,[9] but as registration of NGOs is not mandatory in Senegal, there are likely many more.[10] White SUVs with logos of various aid organizations are omnipresent in Dakar, and the development industry employs thousands of local people not only directly in development programming but also in staff positions, including administrative support, accountants, caseworkers, and the security guards and janitorial staff of offices, as well as the drivers of those SUVs.

In addition to direct local employees of aid agencies, other kinds of workers "are also part of, or gravitate around, the international humanitarian community" (Pascucci 2019, 756) in Dakar. It is the participation of these workers—the nannies, maids, personal chauffeurs, security guards, cooks, and gardeners of aid workers—to whom I turn to explore their role in "the localized economic geographies and political economies of aid" (756). These domestic workers are local workers in the aid economy, if not usually conceived as such. Their reproductive labor makes possible the formal work of international aid practitioners in Dakar and throughout the developing world in ways that are underacknowledged and untheorized.

THE BUBBLE

My fieldwork for this project began before I had conceived of it, when I took a job at a small local NGO in Dakar in 2005 and first began to confront some of the odd dynamics of the international development industry, as well as acquaint myself with the expat bubble in Dakar. Though I had lived in Dakar a few years earlier as a college student studying Wolof and living with a host family, I had spent most of that time immersed in Senegalese family life, socializing in Senegalese homes, with Senegalese friends, and living within the means and rhythms of my host siblings and their friends. I walked or took public transportation everywhere, generally on the bus or a *diaga ndiaye* (white vans that passengers enter and exit through an open back door) or a *kaar rapide* (the colorful vans that are emblematic of Senegal; for a photo, see figure 1, which is in chapter 2). I went dancing with Senegalese friends at neighborhood community-center parties, sat in the stands watching friends play in the Dakar basketball league, and attended weddings, baptisms, and religious festivals in my host sisters' clothes. I was generally the only *toubab* (Wolof for foreigner or white person) in all these settings.

When I returned to Senegal to work in the NGO, I was one of few non-Senegalese employees and by far the youngest person working at the organization. The two American founders of the organization, not-so-Returned Peace Corps Volunteers who had served in West Africa in the 1960s and never went home, had built their health promotion and cultural exchange organization from the ground up. The lingua franca in the office was Wolof, which challenged and delighted me, though most of our formal meetings were held in French. As an impertinent twenty-three-year-old, I made many mistakes interacting with the Senegalese staff—chief among them were my impatience for Senegalese communal norms that made meetings interminable as every person present felt compelled to contribute and my dismissal of the ingrained hierarchies of respect that obliged me to pay deference to all who were older than me (read: everyone on staff) even when I disagreed with them or felt they lacked efficiency in their approach to our work. My smile, sense of humor, and dorky enthusiasm for Wolof language learning went some way to keeping me in the good graces of my colleagues, but in retrospect I also see that as a white American, I was accorded respect that I didn't have to earn. I had a cultural and linguistic shorthand with the American founders of the organization that gave me undue influence from the first days of my employment.

In those years, I was introduced to other Americans and Europeans living in their own expat world in Dakar. Struggling on an unthinkably low salary,[11] I could only dip a toe into this world, but I mixed socially with young journalists for international news organizations and others who had a similarly low-budget style of potluck dinner parties and time on the beach. I was vaguely aware that there was another, fancier expat version of Dakar, but this was brought home to me in the most extreme and absurd way with a chance opportunity to house- and pet-sit for the American ambassador in Dakar. I still don't know how I was identified by the ambassador as a trustworthy person who had nowhere to go and nothing better to do on the holidays, but I gladly accepted her invitation to move into the ambassadorial residence for three weeks to care for the cats she had brought from home and the spirited stray dog she had adopted while in Dakar. This stint in the ambassadorial residence gave me a few weeks of insight into what it was like to have a house full of staff; a cook, a housekeeper, and a "house boy" (who appeared to be in his 60s) all worked in the residence. Though I reveled in what seemed to me to be extremely luxurious accommodations—air conditioning, hot water, wall-to-wall carpet, a washer and dryer—I found living in the presence of the house help deeply uncomfortable. I hated feeling like I was in a fishbowl, observed by all the house staff and unsure of how to behave with them or in front of them. I quickly requested that the cook simply leave things in the little kitchen upstairs for me and go home for the day rather than wait to serve me dinner. I never once used the pool because it seemed there was always someone—a guard, a gardener—walking by on their shift. I never played the grand piano, because I didn't know if I was allowed to and there was generally someone around who might overhear my stuttering sonatas. Out of reluctance to parade my personal business in front of the security guards, I rarely went in or out of the place, except to and from work, nor had visitors.

At one point during my stay, the residence received official visitors—the American ambassador to Burkina Faso and her husband—and I noticed their ease in commanding the staff, marveled as the husband unselfconsciously swam laps in the pool, and wondered if I could ever feel comfortable in this environment. Though most expat aid workers do not have quite such grand accommodations or a fleet of staff as extensive, some shared much in common with the ambassador's way of living in Dakar, as I discovered a few years later.

When I returned to Senegal for anthropological fieldwork during graduate school, I floated on the fringes of a large group of expat development workers who ushered me into their very different Dakar. These new friends lived in furnished apartments with private security (and washer-dryers and air conditioning), had groceries shipped to them from home, took weekend getaways to stay in hotels down the coast, held costume parties, went zip-lining, and ate out regularly in Dakar's beachside restaurants. Many owned cars, had professional wardrobes, and acquired artwork and decorative items at inflated prices from shops catering to their comfort. Most had little interest in immersing themselves in the daily rhythms of Dakar street life and home culture. These friends had acquired the skills they needed for their jobs in development from expensive master's programs and training workshops at "HQ"—there was little to be gained from bumpy rides in a *kaar rapide*.

Most of the aid workers with whom I socialized during this year had been posted to other destinations before their two to three years in Dakar and went on to far-flung posts afterward—to Manila, to South Sudan, to Bangkok. Even while posted in Dakar, some spent several weeks a month traveling for work in the region. Their choice to live very lightly on the surface of Dakar—familiarizing themselves with a handful of restaurants that catered to expats and befriending only other development professionals they might run into years later at a different point in the "aid archipelago" (Duffield 2012)—made sense considering their rotation in this internationally linked geography. As Smirl (2015, 89) notes: "The fundamental quality of this archipelago is its disjuncture with the local physical environment: temporally, socioculturally and in terms of mobility."

The one point with which all these aid workers had connection with local people outside the office was in their employment of domestic workers. All had housekeepers and security guards, at least, and they occasionally discussed with me the awkwardness and gratitude, frustration and resentment that characterized their relationships with these domestic employees.

By this time, I was living with a Senegalese friend who was working as a domestic worker for an American family. Through my roommate and her friends and fellow domestic workers as they navigated complicated dynamics with their employers, I gained access to another perspective on expats and their impact in Dakar. My roommate and her friends did not see themselves as participating in the development industry nor did they see the development industry as having a transformative impact on their lives. They did, however, feel they were learning a great deal about the cultural life of toubabs and the rewards of relative extreme wealth and privileged mobility—all while their reproductive labor allowed their employers to ostensibly work to eradicate poverty for the citizens of their county.

Analysis of relations between aid workers and their domestic workers is critical for an understanding of how people in countries targeted by development experience its structures and practices in daily life. Séverine Autesserre (2014, 28–29) rightly notes that the daily lives of humanitarian workers in the field are just as relevant to local people's understanding and evaluation of international interventions as the humanitarian work they are doing. Employing domestic helpers is one key way in which expat development workers impact local lives. These positions provide a livelihood for the people they employ, but they also send profound messages about the resource gap between expats and locals and the racial and national hierarchies of global political economy. How do big, fancy houses and very visible conspicuous consumption, including the consumption of care, serve as a walking confirmation and normalization of what Trouillot called "the universal legitimacy of European—and racialized white—

power" (1991, 32)? For expat aid workers brought to Senegal to create programming discouraging economic migration, for example, the very presence of Western aid workers and their comparative wealth and visible consumption practices might be productively examined as a counterpoint to the messaging of their work. Ethnographers of development have insisted that policy is not made in the tidy offices of experts, but that it becomes what it is during implementation.[12] I contend that this includes the way that expat aid workers live, play, and solicit paid care in their overseas posts.

THE AID INDUSTRY

Though many critiques of development focus on development's ineffectiveness—programs that fail to reach their stated goals and the collective failure of an industry that has certainly fallen short of its aim of eliminating poverty—Ferguson (1994, 254) has suggested that what is perhaps most important about development projects is not so much their regular inability to meet their objectives as their unintended effects.[13] One meaningful effect of the development industry is the outsized compensation that expat aid workers receive and its relative obscenity next to conditions of poverty among which they live,[14] not to mention the racial privilege, power and status they often possess in the places where they are posted (Pierre 2013). These are visible manifestations and performances of a racialized world order in which whiteness is the embodiment of development, modernity, wealth, and power.[15]

Indeed, the foundational concepts of "developed" and "underdeveloped" are not objective categorizations; they are man-made designations whose history is rooted in a colonial understanding of the world as organized by a split between civility and primitivity.[16] The conceit of development presumes a ladder to modernity on which certain countries are at the top and others are at the bottom.[17] The "development" metaphor itself is a biological one: poor people should "develop" from childhood (poverty) into adulthood (prosperity).[18]

The vernacular of development is, as Jemima Pierre convincingly argues, a "racial vernacular" whose very terminology works to "reinforce patterns of racial (dis)advantage, global inequality, and relations structured in dominance" (2020, 87).

The technocratic terminology of development acts explicitly to depoliticize poverty and obscure its racial ideology, as so many anthropologists of development have argued.[19] That Western development experts have tools to "build capacity" in poorer countries that simply lack the tools for their own advancement suggests a kind of racialized superiority still visible in the power distribution within the international aid industry.[20] Such white-dominated power structures, as well as a technocratic approach that attempts to obscure it, has meant that "poverty, illiteracy, and even hunger became the basis of a lucrative industry for planners, experts, and civil servants," largely from the Global North (Escobar 1999, 385).[21] Escobar credits the creation of this lucrative industry as the only real success of development work; the "problems" of global poverty still exist, while the development industry thrives, with master's programs in development practice proliferating in the West and a steady offering of jobs for the technicians of poverty management. The development industry has effectively developed systematized classifications that "call" for solutions and for practitioners to work on solving them, with technical skills equally applicable in Lahore or Lesotho—and with very few consequences for the practitioners if the programs fail.

This reminds us that the development industry itself is just one engine of global capitalism in which the global inequalities of race, nationality, and gender are not neutralized but are in many ways reproduced and heightened. Again, following Hannah Appel (2019), it is not enough to say, "Ha! Development doesn't work!" because it has not eradicated poverty, because most countries that were deemed "developing" have not transitioned into "developed," because the Millennium Development Goals did not meet their targets and with remarkably undiminished self-confidence were rebranded as Sustainable Development Goals and kept on plugging. Development does work. It is incredibly productive in upholding a global social order, redolent of colonial aromas, where knowledge and power are situated in particular places and are of a particular hue.

RACE, COLONIALISM, AND A CASTED LABOR SYSTEM

Though the ethnographic focus in this study is on the hypermobile middle-class experts of international development, there is a growing group that has only begun to draw scholarly attention, the "subordinate development professionals" (Heathershaw 2016, 79) hired on local contract who make up a large proportion of the development industry (Pascucci 2019; Egeland et al. 2011, 31). It is not surprising that this industry that is "structured around hierarchies of race and place" (Pailey 2021, 32) should contain profound inequities between local workers and expat or "international" staff. A nuanced exploration of these inequities is the subject of an increasing body of scholarship.[22]

Rebecca Warne Peters opines that within the development industry's hierarchy of personnel, "deciding what to do becomes the component presumed to require real skill and expertise, presumably foreign, while carrying out what has been decided is presumed to be the work of mere practice, performable by undifferentiated masses of national staff" (2020, 20). In other words, expatriate aid workers are privileged as the all-important "deciders," and the local staff are mere doers.[23] They are compensated as such, with international staff receiving not only exponentially higher salaries but also considerable perks and amenities that can include housing, private security, relocation costs, and copious paid leave. The important skill sets that local aid workers offer, "being specialists who understand the history, culture, and fast-moving politics of a place" (Slim 1995, 121), are far from valued by the aid industry, and the symbols of expertise in this hierarchy of knowledge are qualifications that people from the Global South have significantly more difficulty accessing.[24] One example is extensive international experience, which is much simpler to accrue for those not facing extensive visa restrictions due to their citizenship.[25] As a result of this coding of only certain qualifications and provenances as valuable expertise, local aid workers are given relatively limited authority, pay, and professional mobility. As others have argued, this creates a dynamic that is not only unjust but unproductive: expatriates believe they already have the answers they need and therefore are not incentivized to improve their understandings of local circumstances, leading to ineffective programming, while local staff members get demotivated and devalue their own experience.[26] With these dynamics and the massive disparities in salary and compensation for local versus international staff, the development industry works to uphold the status quo of a profoundly uneven global division of labor, mobility, and consumption.

Though it no longer feels like "breaking a taboo" to speak of race in development to the extent that it seemed twenty years ago (White 2002, 407), much development scholarship and programming remains obstinately color-blind.[27] Development still suffers from what Pailey (2020) calls the "white gaze" problem. The depoliticization and deracialization of discourses of poverty and development insidiously frame continued power imbalances as being outside racial dynamics while perpetuating them. This allows practitioners and scholars of development to be silent on questions of race and therefore to avoid confronting the uncomfortable reality of the "the powers, privileges and inequalities that continue to flow from whiteness" (Pailey 2021, 732).

International aid professionals, like most professionals, are engaged in "crafting comfortable lives" (Fechter 2012, 1483) for themselves. Aid itself can be a lifestyle choice, one that at a certain level entails a good salary, international travel, and an opportunity for enhanced status. Although expat aid workers make significant sacrifices in moving overseas for work—being far from extended family and dealing with frustrating infrastructural challenges are among their chief complaints—they also reap tremendous benefits in their expat lifestyles that throw into relief the fundamental and enduring global inequalities that are so crucial to the survival and propagation of the aid industry. One of these benefits is being able to live at a level of social standing far above those around you.

Because expat development workers usually earn "10, 20, sometimes even 100 times the local salary" (McWha-Hermann 2011, 30), they have the ability to live well above their comparative station in their homeland. This is by no means a new critique; books like Graham Hancock's *Lords of Poverty* have spoken to the fact that money earmarked for alleviating poverty "pays the hefty salaries and underwrites the privileged lifestyles of the international civil servants, 'development experts,' consultants and assorted freeloaders who staff the aid agencies themselves" (1989, iii). Ross Coggin's famous, mercilessly sarcastic poem "The Development Set" (1978) offers a depiction of aid workers as self-righteous and out-of-touch grifters, enriching themselves with a smug sense of their own saintly goodness:

> *We discuss malnutrition over steaks*
> *And plan hunger talks during coffee breaks.*
> *Whether Asian floods or African drought,*
> *We face each issue with open mouth.*
>
> *We bring in consultants whose circumlocution*
> *Raises difficulties for every solution—*
> *Thus guaranteeing continued good eating*
> *By showing the need for another meeting.*

Focusing on how aid workers profit from their aid work can be awkward or uncomfortable because of the perceived "moral untouchability of humanitarianism" (Fassin 2011) and commonly held conceptions of aid workers as altruists (Shutt 2012, 1532; Fechter 2012). Pointing out the financial and personal advantages they gain through their work disrupts such conceptions. It can seem like a moral indictment when I describe, for example, the Greek UN junior program officer I knew in Dakar who dedicated a bedroom of her house to be the hookah room for hookah parties with her aid worker friends because the house she had been assigned had more bedrooms than she knew what to do with, or when I discuss the French employee of a maternal and child health NGO whose weekend routine was to pay for a day pass for her family of three to spend the day by the pool of a luxury hotel even though their own apartment building also had a pool.[28] Yet, development agencies incorporate the expectation of a certain lifestyle into their salaries and expat perk packages. "Living well" while "doing good" (Fechter 2012) is built into the model of the development industry for expats.

A key amenity of being an expat in the developing world is the access to incredibly cheap domestic labor. My interviewees in Dakar were able to afford a level of household help that they were the first to exclaim they could never have imagined in their home county. Full-time nannies; housekeepers who cook, shop, and run errands; drivers who escort your children to and from school—these were services that only the ultra-wealthy could afford back home in France, Holland, or the US. This cheaply purchased care work, they noted, not only made life easier for them but, especially for female aid workers, allowed a work-life balance that has become almost mythical for professionals at home. Freed from domestic responsibilities, they could not only "lean in" at work but have time for leisure, pleasure, exercise, and quality time with spouses, friends, and kids.[29] The production/ reproduction of their class status and privilege was contingent on the abundance of low-wage labor of local people and their exploitation of that labor.

CARE AND EXTRACTION

This book relies on a feminist ethics of care, what Tara Patricia Cookson describes as "an approach to understanding the world that recognizes the centrality of caring to healthy and productive individuals and societies" (2018, 24). In the following chapters, I examine themes of care and caring through multiple registers at once. Any discussion about hired domestic work is necessarily a discussion about care: the paradoxes in valuation of care, our ambivalent attitude toward care, our commodification of care.

Much of the literature on the extraction of care and on care work across citizenship has been about migrant care workers and local employers. The dynamic in this book is the reverse. As Senegalese nannies raise expat children, as Senegalese *guardiens* protect the homes and property of expat employers, as Senegalese maids cook, clean, shop, and cater to the needs of expats, they are performing caring labor for migrants. Expatriates abroad are often rendered childlike in their inability to accomplish correctly the most modest of domestic goals by the standards of those around them. In a new location with a foreign language and customs, shopping for groceries or finding a locksmith can be intimidating and confusing. In their helplessness, expats rely on domestic staff generally for much more than the ostensible labors in a job description.

But this care relation between aid workers and their domestic staff is not unidirectional. Many of my expat aid-worker interlocutors perceive of their employment of local domestic workers as a matter of care. Numerous aid workers framed their employment of house helpers as a moral obligation—creating jobs in a country of low employment, paying salaries above the local rate with better working conditions. Aid workers discussed with me their projects for improving the lives of their workers; these projects went beyond monthly salaries and into paying school fees for their workers' children, giving them life advice, teaching them new skills that could help them economically, and then finding them a new job after the aid workers move on to their next post. Like aid agencies to villages or states, they magisterially decided in which aspects of life to invest their resources, using their own criteria to evaluate the domestic workers' biggest and most worthy needs.

Erica Bornstein provides a model for looking at care on several registers at once. In *Disquieting Gifts* (2012), she connects the dots between development, charity, and humanitarianism—usually seen to be separate realms. Following the lives of people in New Delhi, she gives attention to the "spontaneous, informal, unmediated, and habitual" humanitarian gestures that don't make headlines (174). Giving to a beggar or sending money to an NGO may not be considered humanitarian work, but they are parallel gestures that make meaning for the givers and the receivers. Care itself can confirm or construct positions of superiority and inferiority, intentionally or unintentionally (Drotbohm 2015, 111), and acts of charity are no exception. Though capricious and temporary, subject to the will of the donor, they nonetheless "challenge people to think relationally about their place in the world" (Bornstein 2012, 172). This relationality is key to understanding the dynamics between aid work and care work as well. As I argue in chapter 4, for many development workers, treating their own employment of low-wage domestic labor as a development project was crucial to reconciling the glaring inconsistencies between their understandings of the altruism that brought them to Africa and the material rewards they reaped by being there.

Domestic work is usually categorized as intimate labor, not because the relations between domestic employees and their employers are always emotionally close—though of course some are—but because the labor of a domestic employee takes place within the intimate space of the home. Boris and Parreñas categorize intimate labor as "work that involves embodied and affective interactions in the service of social reproduction" (2010, 7), drawing on Evelyn Nakano Glenn's definition of social reproduction as "the array of activities and relationships involved in maintaining people both on a daily basis and intergenerationally" (1992, 1). They further define intimate labor as work that "involves tending to the intimate needs of individuals, work that exposes personal information that would leave one vulnerable if others had access to such knowledge" (Boris and Parreñas 2010,

5). Nannies, maids, security guards, and drivers all participate in and are witness to the private and the intimate. The maids I interviewed know where the cash is kept in the home, which development workers drink to excess, how and how much their employers eat, how they discipline their children, and so on. Security guards know who visits at night, who stays out dancing until dawn, and who plays hooky from work. Each of these workers is necessarily brought into the personal life of the employer in ways that are often uncomfortably intimate.

In many contexts, employers and employees must navigate these complicated and sometimes unwelcome intimacies though various forms of boundary work (Lan 2003). These include the usage of fictive kin idioms (Nguyen 2014), creating physical or ritual distance (Lan 2003), "soft violence" (Parreñas, Kantachote, and Silvey 2020), and bargaining and reasserting power dynamics through making and breaking "ground rules" (Yeoh and Huang 2010). For Senegalese maids and their expat employers, these negotiations of power and intimacy come in multiple forms that include many of the above as well as invocations of care and appeals to the paternalistic expectation of magnanimous care for the world's poor from the West that undergird the foundation of international development.

Development work, too, is often framed as a matter of care. Aid workers, as well as the world at large, usually see their contribution as caring for the world's poor, as providing help and "aid." There is, of course, a marked paternalism baked into this framing, as Western expatriates are positioned as the caretaking adults, and beneficiaries of aid as the helpless children.[30] Care here is not conceived of as a benignly positive or even value-neutral force or instinct; projects and regimes of caring can often serve colonizing ends and perpetuate or cement inequalities.[31] After all, "the politics of caring have been at the heart of concerns with exclusions and critiques of power dynamics in stratified worlds" (de la Bellacasa 2011, 86).

The parallels to colonial interpretations of intervention as care abound on this point. One can draw a line from the *mission civila-*

trice of French colonialism to contemporary development objectives and rhetoric that operate in former colonies.[32] The ideals of the *mission civilatrice*—that it was France's moral duty as a superior population with demonstrated successes in economic, medical, and political realms to uplift the inferior races (Conklin 1997)—map all too neatly onto the caring rhetoric of contemporary development. Save the Children, CARE International, and other major aid organizations that offer "solutions" and "relief" to the global poor invoke a sense of duty to help that preserves the assumption that to have resources is equivalent to having knowledge and wisdom to impart to those who, having fewer resources, are assumed to be lacking in knowledge and wisdom.

As Michelle Murphy so eloquently puts it, "The stratigraphies of care, intimate relations, and labor have long legacies that thread through the very operation of European colonialism and American slavery, segregation, and empire" (2015, 724). In West Africa, in the postwar period of French colonialism in particular, there was a distinct turn to focus rhetorically on the good works of colonialism. This period—referred to as "welfare colonialism" by Young (1994) or even "developmental colonialism" by Cooper (2002)—put a charitable face on imperialism in large part in response to the growing criticism of colonialism at home and in the colonies (Beeckmans 2017, 360). A strategic rebranding focused on benevolent projects of lifting people up, rather than on the realities of labor extraction (including military labor in the form of soldiers) and resource extraction. In Africa and beyond, these "humanitarian 'good works' of empire were part of its very durable architecture—with exacting exclusions and inequities structured through them" (Stoler 2010, xii).

In focusing on the relationship between development work and domestic work in this book, I am similarly interested in the contemporary labor and resource extraction that a charitable face can obscure. My study's focus on the care work of local people *for* expatriate aid workers flips the script on facile representations of Western aid workers coming to help, emphasizing instead the reproductive labor of local people that upholds the international development industry.

All these conversations (on neocolonialism, equity, and race) are conversations aid workers are already having in online forums, in industry newsletters, and around the water cooler. Expat professionals of color, especially those who come from the Global South, have moved conversations forward on these topics within aid worker circles, though they lament the pushback or empty lip service that often greets their efforts. A key point I try to stress in this book is that most present-day expatriate aid workers are not clueless parodies of colonial officials going through the motions with nothing but contempt or paternalistic condescension to the populations they serve. The majority of aid workers I spent time with and interviewed were politically engaged, moderate liberals who abhorred racism in the abstract and talked about poverty as a structural global system of inequality. Most were concerned about inequity in their own lives, and this had multiple and diverse ramifications for their relations with their domestic staff. Yet the pervasiveness of the development industry's bent toward reinforcing the global social order takes much of the teeth out of these individual reckonings. There is a great deal of talk about the development industry's ultimate goal being "to put itself out of business," ostensibly by "solving" global poverty, but the reality is that it continues to be a lucrative industry for Western professionals who benefit individually and as an industry from the perpetuation of the global status quo.

RESEARCH METHODS

This book is based on multiple years of participant observation in expat Dakar over the past decade and a half, five years of digital ethnography in expat and aid worker online spaces, and a core of thirty-six ethnographic interviews conducted between December 2016 and January 2019 with both expat aid workers in Dakar, Senegal, (in French, Italian and English) and with their domestic employees (in French and Wolof), as well as other Senegalese who work in and around development, and development workers now stationed in the US.

My participant observation spanned my many different iterations as an American in Dakar before my targeted research on this
project: first as an undergraduate student in a family homestay, then
as an employee of a local NGO, and subsequently as a doctoral student researching marriage and migration. Those diverse experiences
brought me into contact with vastly different aspects of expat life in
the city and gave me a longitudinal perspective as the city grew and
changed. From 2015 to 2019, I returned to Dakar several times for
more concentrated fieldwork on expat life in Dakar in businesses catering to expats, in expat homes, and in the homes of domestic workers for expats.

My digital research was conducted through blogs and social
media groups of self-proclaimed expatriates and aid workers. Facebook groups like AidMamas, AidBnb, and 50Shades of Aid are
active places of connection and information-sharing for those working in the aid industry. Posts about job interviews, development tool
kits, and current events are interspersed with very personal queries
about life as an expatriate aid worker. Other Facebook groups cater to
a wider and more vaguely defined expat identity, like Grumpy Expat,
which is mostly ornery complaints along the lines of "Why don't
people in this country understand how to do this simple thing properly like we do at home!?" A number of Senegal-specific Facebook
groups cater to expat conversations, though they are populated by
Senegalese as well, from ELVIS (Expats, Locals and Visitors in Senegal) to the food-focused Dakar Eats and the fashion-focused Gazelle
Skirt. Parenting groups like Super Parents de Dakar share resources
on activities for children, pediatricians, and others; classified-ad
groups like Dakarium's Housing Staff page post and respond to ads
for domestic workers. As a participant observer in all these groups, I
found that hiring, firing, training and managing domestic workers
are frequent topics of posts and threads, and I have mined them as
sources of "convergent data" (Geertz 1982, 156) on this topic.

In my ethnographic interviews in Senegal, I was able to ask questions
grounded in the many dynamics that I had observed and confronted

in my years in Dakar. Respondents were identified through snowball sampling and using my social networks developed over years of working and living in Dakar. The majority of expat interviewees were from France and the US; the remainder were from other parts of Europe and the Americas. The aid workers ranged in age from their early thirties to their mid-fifties. These aid workers worked for a range of different kinds of development organizations. Some were employees of a Western government's development agency who had their housing paid for and maintained (and sometimes furnished) by their home government. Others worked for the UN or a large international NGO with expatriate salary packages that included housing assistance, funds to pay for their children's schooling, and relocation costs. Some worked for smaller local NGOs with considerably more modest operating budgets and fewer frills, and a few were hired on local contracts with international agencies or as consultants for specific projects with international agencies. Their jobs ranged from managing regional infrastructure programs to implementing village-based water and sanitation projects.

My formal interviews with Senegalese domestic workers employed by aid workers were conducted separately from their employers. Their duties were myriad, but the majority defined themselves as maids, nannies, or cooks, and occasionally all three. Their ages ran from mid-twenties to late fifties. All but one had previously been employed by expats, and about half had also worked as maids in Senegalese households before making the jump to work for expatriates.

My previous experience of years of living as an expat in Dakar and my familiarity with the dynamics and landscapes of the expat lifestyle in the city gave me immediate access to an understanding that facilitated my interviews with expat workers. My fluency in Wolof, my considerable familiarity with Senegalese culture and tradition as an anthropologist of Senegal, and my close connections to Senegalese family and friends set me apart from other expats in Senegal and allowed me to connect with domestic worker interviewees as we broached potentially uncomfortable subjects, such as the habits and characteristics of toubabs and their households.

It goes without saying that my citizenship and race inevitably shaped my research and writing. My access to the research and participants was shaped in various ways by race and privilege. A US passport in Africa (and elsewhere in the developing world) is like a talisman against all kinds of trouble. Mine allowed me, first and foremost, to travel back and forth to Senegal with little trouble or forethought, something African anthropologists of Europe or the US do not enjoy. It also felt like a get-out-of-jail-free card of sorts, allowing me to feel confident and protected in my status. In Senegal, its presence is implied by my whiteness. A colonial legacy of white supremacy in Senegal allows me to move freely about Dakar, ask impertinent questions, break social rules, have taxi cabs stop for me day and night, and confidently take up space in a country not my own. As Jemima Pierre argues of Ghana, whiteness in nominally postcolonial Senegal continues to have tremendous currency, "revealing a clear discourse of race that is articulated through practices that both reflect global economic, political, and cultural hierarchies and also reinforce white privilege on the local level" (2013, 112).

My race and citizenship opened doors in conducting interviews. With expats, my skin and my nationality made me an unthreatening, immediately sympathetic interlocutor. Just as in earlier years, expat professional aid workers welcomed me into their social circles, entrusted their pets to me, and let me stay in their homes when they were gone despite our limited acquaintance and without so much as a cursory background check. In conducting interviews for this project, my whiteness in a non-white context literally and figuratively got me in the door. It meant people opened their homes to me, invited me to cocktails and dinners, and talked with me openly about many topics, including race. Their security guards saw me as nonthreatening and admitted me into their employers' buildings and homes with little resistance upon my first visit, even if they had not been alerted in advance to my arrival. My age at the time I conducted interviews for this project, in my thirties, also made me the counterpart of many of the aid worker interviewees—a young professional woman, a working mother, a person with experience in development work and international travel, an ostensibly liberal and "woke" person with whom they shared a shorthand and a benefit of the doubt when they said problematic things with a wink.

With domestic workers, my skin color afforded me an undue level of respect and authority that both granted me access and was sometimes a liability in earning their direct confidence. I sought to mitigate that liability with my fluency in Wolof, knowledge of Senegalese culture, and connections to Senegalese people in their personal networks, yet my race and citizenship and therefore my relative power was never erased by these tactics.

IN WHAT FOLLOWS . . .

This book follows a string of studies in the anthropology of development that put the spotlight on a group that was largely missing from anthropological examinations of development: aid workers themselves. Though older analyses brought important insights through examination of policy and its implementation,[33] the emergence of development as an idea,[34] and aid recipients as ethnographic subjects,[35] this newer literature shifts the focus onto aid workers and their lives.[36] Elizabeth Harrison's critique of the literature of "Aidland" argues that its potential for navel-gazing obscures relations of power within aid, but her critique imagines that power is only in play in the "processes of aid delivery" and in "development outcomes" (2013, 271) and that these are somehow separate from the aid workers themselves. In direct contradiction to this notion, this book draws from a long tradition within feminist scholarship to argue that there is no such separation between politics and domesticity and uses the domestic lives of aid workers explicitly as a means for an analysis of power.

In the following chapter, I discuss the specifics of the domestic worker marketplace in Dakar. Though the exploitation of domestic workers has become a focal point of development intervention globally, the practices of development workers as employers of domestic labor remain ignored and unspoken. Through an analysis of social media posts and classified ads soliciting and offering domestic labor, as well as interviews with aid worker employers and domestic workers, I detail the basic contours of the informal but routine process of recruiting and hiring a domestic worker in Dakar, the expectations of employers versus employees, and the implications of an informal labor sector and a rotating door of transient employers for the precarity of domestic workers.

Chapter 2 explores the role of security in the domestic life of expat aid workers in Senegal. Within the framework of increased securitization that defines contemporary aid work, I show that fears about security, especially material security, shape how expat aid workers live and behave in Dakar. I argue that concerns with security create a distance between expat aid workers and those around them more generally. Expat aid workers develop everyday bordering practices to mitigate their vulnerability, and these practices have implications for the residential geography of Dakar, as well as how aid workers interact with those closest to them physically, their domestic staff.

In Senegal, not only expats hire domestic service. It is commonplace for elite Senegalese to hire drivers and gardeners; most middle-class and even lower-middle-class Dakar families employ maids or at least laundresses. Men and women hired as domestic workers for Senegalese households in Dakar generally hail from rural Senegal, part of a larger rural-to-urban labor migration that was a result of structural adjustment programs and a series of severe droughts in the 1970s and 1980s. In chapter 3, I explore the theme of migration and mobility, arguing that both domestic employee and employer are, in essence, economic migrants. Moving from one part of the world to another, explicitly in search of work that allows for a better quality of living, is economic migration. Race and colonial legacy often prevent scholars, governments and laypeople from categorizing expatriates from the West to the developing world in this manner,[37] but their transnationalism is a constitutive part of postcolonial mobility that merits analytical attention.[38] The discrepancy in the mobility of aid workers and domestic workers that I highlight in this chapter and in their relative ability to prevent precarity underlines the mismatched rewards of development to its practitioners and supposed beneficiaries.

Chapter 4 probes the ambivalent feelings that expat aid workers have about their domestic workers and about the work contracted between them. In the chapter, I look at three strategies that aid workers employ to recast their purchase of cheap domestic labor as an act more in line with their self-image as humanitarians. By positioning themselves as job creators, nice friendly bosses, and capacity-building developers of their domestic employees, aid workers seek to ignore or minimize class and racial discomfort through idioms of care. These tactics make individual aid workers feel more comfortable, but do little to alter the tremendous power imbalances and wealth disparities that allow them to move to a poor country and purchase a level of caring labor they could not afford back home.

In the book's conclusion, I turn to the growing call for a reexamination of the hierarchies within international development work. A burgeoning movement seeks to upset the existing model of expatriate supremacy in aid work and argues for the decolonization of the development sector. The conclusion engages with this movement and with the critiques of development that argue that the "chronic mobility" and high turnover rate of development as currently structured is highly inefficient and unsustainable.[39] I propose a more honest reckoning of the true beneficiaries of development as an industry.

1 | FINDING HELP IN THE INFORMAL ECONOMY

DURING MY FIELDWORK IN DAKAR, I met with Odile, a Senegalese employee of the International Organization of Migration (IOM) who works on domestic workers' rights. As we sat down for coffee in a café across the street from her office building, I told her about my research project on domestic workers. She launched immediately into a detailed explanation of the work that the IOM was doing for Senegalese women who had been trafficked as domestic workers to the Middle East. She and her team were coordinating between Senegalese government officials and the governments of countries where the women were trafficked into labor, helping release the women from their abusive circumstances and return them home to Senegal. This work was part of a larger IOM movement to recognize and address the precarious circumstances and exploitation of migrant domestic workers across the world, including issuing guidelines for the ethical recruitment of domestic workers, conducting research into the connection between child trafficking and domestic service, and creating programming around International Domestic Workers' Day.[1] I listened with interest, then tried to shift the conversation to my own research subject. Did Odile have thoughts about domestic workers working in Senegal, particularly for people like her expat colleagues at the IOM?

Odile told me the story of her own cousin whom she had recommended to a French development worker looking for a maid. The cousin quit after two months of mistreatment, complaining that her boss allowed her to eat only leftovers and refused to let her drink from the family's water glasses. " 'I was using my hand!' " Odile recalls her cousin exclaiming when she called to announce that she was leaving her job. "She did not have the right to drink filtered water, and she did not have the right to drink from the cups."[2] This indignity eventually pushed Odile's cousin to leave her job despite what she considered a decent salary and acceptable hours.

Odile and I discussed whether development workers ever think about the rights of domestic workers in terms of their own household employees. She confessed that even though her colleagues should ideally sign formal contracts with their domestic workers, she has never asked her colleagues if they do. The idea of asking them about their own practices as employers of domestic labor had never occurred to her, despite her role as an expert in domestic workers' rights. She said furthermore that she would be hesitant to ever do so, "because it's something that happens in the private circle. . . . So people do not want to talk about it. For them, it's private."

Part of what makes domestic work so difficult to regulate and makes domestic workers vulnerable to exploitation and abuse is its confinement to the private sphere. Only recently have activists and scholars begun to bring domestic labor into public conversations about human rights and labor law. Domestic labor is now the target of more and more development industry interventions; new charters and treaties hold nations accountable for protecting the rights of domestic workers; NGOs attempt to reach out to domestic workers to educate them of their rights and protections as workers and, often, as migrants. Domestic work is increasingly a matter professional importance to development organizations. Within the ranks of development workers, however, it remains a private issue, a taboo topic that even specialists like Odile feel would be inappropriate to address with co-workers.

In this chapter, I dig into the nuts and bolts of expat aid workers' private employment of domestic workers, including recruitment, job expectations, and payment. As this chapter makes clear, expatriates generally do not hire domestics as formal employees. As in most other contexts of domestic service for hire, there is little to no supervision or regulation of the working conditions for domestic employees and few consequences for the employers if they do not adhere to local labor laws or practices. When aid workers inevitably leave their post after a few years, though they often informally try to find a new situation for the domestic worker through classified ads and their personal networks, there are few consequences for the employer if they cannot, but there are potentially severe consequences for the domestic worker facing unemployment.

RECRUITMENT

"How did you find your maid?" was a question I asked all the aid workers I interviewed. Their responses varied but cohered around a few common avenues. As in other locations where aid workers are stationed, there are multiple channels for finding domestic workers in Dakar. There are formal agencies where domestic workers are supposedly vetted and trained; these take either a flat fee or a percentage of the monthly salary as their compensation for this brokering. Few of the aid workers I knew and interviewed had opted for this service in Dakar, however, although several had used an agency in other posts. These agencies had a bad reputation in Dakar's expat social media groups for falsifying or exaggerating their employees' skills and experience. People in these forums specifically complained that they were sent domestic workers who clearly had no training or experience working in expatriate households after being given inflated employment histories.

Because experience in expatriate households is so precious, for reasons that become clearer below, aid workers generally utilize more informal channels to find domestic employees. They usually follow one of three paths. The first is to use their personal network of fellow expats and aid workers to find a suitable employee or to "inherit" a worker from a previous expat colleague from their office, a previous expat tenant of their house or apartment, or an expat friend who is leaving the country, off to the next mission. A second common route is to have one domestic worker use his or her personal and professional networks to find additional employees—for example, a nanny recommending a sister or a friend as a housekeeper for the employer's family. The third common avenue through which expats aid workers find their domestic worker is via an advertisement posted in a newsletter or social media site by another expat, like the ad that opens the introduction to this book.

DE BOUCHE À L'OREILLE

In a climate where trust is paramount, for a position in the intimate domestic sphere of the home, recommendations from peers and old friends matter a great deal. It is unsurprising, then, that personal recommendations of domestic employees from friends—even if it has been years since their stay in Dakar—weigh more heavily than other considerations when aid workers hire domestic staff. Because the world of aid is relatively small and because of the familiar routes of "the aid archipelago" (Duffield 2012) on which Dakar a common stop, it was not unusual for aid workers to have friends or acquaintances who had been posted to Dakar. They were thus beneficiaries of a transnational informal network of domestic worker recommendations.

Amanda, an American who works for an international NGO in nutrition and food security, reached deeply into her aid network to find a nanny for her new baby. The father of a graduate school friend recommended his housekeeper from his time in Dakar with his NGO six years earlier. Amanda interviewed other women as well but said the personal connection to people she knew and trusted was a large reason she hired this woman. "I got really excited about that connection and just knowing that they really loved her. And she's still in touch with them, like emails with them. So yeah, that was a big part of it." Hiring a domestic worker is risky not only from a security perspective but also because of the potential awkwardness of having a stranger in your home. This connection made the new nanny not a stranger but a friend of a friend.

In contrast to how she found her nanny, Amanda's search for a maid was more serendipitous. As she put it, a housekeeper "just fell into my lap." A friend, another American aid worker in Dakar, had a part-time cleaner who had recently lost her other part-time cleaning job for an expat family when that family decided they needed a full-time employee. The friend suggested that Amanda might hire her to come clean for the two days she was now free.

Gemma, an employee of USAID, also used her aid worker networks to find her housekeeper. At a barbeque in Washington, DC, the summer before she and her family of four moved to Dakar, they ran into American friends Gemma had known through her work in the Peace Corps in Mali many years earlier. These friends had coincidentally lived in the south of Senegal for five years[3] and recommended their beloved housekeeper. Gemma and her husband interviewed other women as well but ended up hiring their friends' former employee, despite some reservations about the quality of her work.

Sylvie, a French employee of an organization that focuses on maternal and child health, twice relied on word-of-mouth guidance ("de bouche à l'oreille," as she put it) from friends in her search for suitable nannies. She, too, had friends who had previously lived in Senegal and who recommended their nanny. That nanny was already employed with another family, but she recommended her sister, whom they hired. After a trial period, they concluded that the sister was too inexperienced to care for their young child and found her unmotivated and easily fatigued. By that point they had met another French couple who had been in Dakar for several years. That couple's nanny had a friend with nineteen years of experience working with expats who was currently unemployed, and she became Sylvie's nanny.

As the above case makes clear, domestic workers, too, use this kind of informal *bouche à l'oreille* network, finding work through their siblings, friends, and former classmates. Many of the domestic workers I interviewed were first connected to expat employers through their friends. Ndeye, a nanny for an American family, got her first job with American aid workers through her friend Adama, who had been their nanny for two years. When Adama's previous employer offered to bring her to the US to work for them there, she asked Ndeye to take over her current job so she could migrate. Ndeye readily agreed and left her position with a Senegalese family.

When an Irish expat named Fiona went back to work for a large religious development organization, she hired a second person to help with housework so that Florence, her primary *nounou*, as she referred to her, could devote herself entirely to the children and the cooking. The first housekeeper Fiona hired did not work out because she and Florence did not get along. As Fiona recounted it, that woman eventually "went to another family and was amazingly happy." Then Florence proposed someone else to work as the housekeeper—in fact, her own housekeeper, Aminata. "It was kind of weird," Fiona admitted. "But she said, 'I can vouch for her,' and I said, 'Okay, I trust you.' And they're like sisters. Everyone has a very good dynamic."

Madeleine had worked as a nanny and a maid for expat families for several decades, and her employment trajectory illustrates how much referrals, both from her Senegalese networks and between expat employers, play a role in creating and impeding employment opportunities. Before she worked for aid workers, Madeleine worked for the French head of Dakar's port and his family until his departure from Senegal in 2004. At that time, a maid she knew who worked in a neighboring home heard of a job opening and recommended her to an American executive director of some type of development program who had just arrived with his family. Before she could begin working for them, however, the family suddenly withdrew their offer of employment because a friend of the executive director's wife had instructed them to take her maid's cousin as their maid instead. As a consolation, the American executive director recommended Madeleine to his deputy, who had just moved to town from the US and was staying in a downtown hotel with her mother and her children until they could move into the lodgings provided by her employer.

The newly arrived deputy asked Madeleine to work with the kids for a fifteen-day trial at the hotel. Although Madeleine got along well with the children, word of mouth once again got in the way. During her stay in the hotel, the deputy bumped into a former colleague whom she'd worked with at a previous post, who put her in touch with her own former maid. The deputy took this recommendation and hired that woman instead. Madeleine was paid for the fifteen days of work but was left without a job once again.

During those fifteen days, however, the executive director's family had let their maid go, unsatisfied with her work, so they asked Madeleine to do a trial day at their home. At the end of that day, they hired her and she worked with them for the next five months. As we sat in the kitchen of the bright and airy apartment of the American man for whom she now worked, Madeleine, a fervent Catholic, told me she thought that her shuffling between these employers was part of God's plan. After five months, the executive director and his deputy both left their positions unexpectedly. Madeleine worked for her boss's replacement; the deputy was not replaced. For Madeleine, God had arranged things so that she would have a next job when her boss departed early, unlike the deputy's housekeeper who was left without employment.

As she took a break from her cleaning to chat with me, Madeleine continued to enumerate the succession of other expat families she worked for after that replacement, each of whom stayed for less than four years. She noted how fortunate she was that each of them found her another position when they left at the end of their mission, with gaps of only a few months between jobs. Even a family who fired her, for reasons that to her are still unclear, found her another family to work for after letting her go.

Most domestic workers emphasize the precarity of their position. They find themselves dependent on the goodwill and satisfaction of their employers not only to remain employed under them but for their subsequent employment when their expat bosses inevitably leave for their next mission somewhere else in the world. Because expats' recommendations to one another were given such importance in hiring, a glowing or mediocre recommendation from a departing employer could mean the difference between continued financial solvency and a long period of zero income. Domestic workers relied heavily on their bosses advocating for them to secure a new gig upon their departure and this shaped their power in setting limits and boundaries with their employers about their hours, pay, and working conditions.

TAKE MY NANNY, PLEASE!

For those expats who arrive in Dakar with no leads from their personal or professional networks, online fora and social media groups take the place of word-of-mouth channels. The specific resources aid workers consult depend to some extent on language and nationality. Many American aid workers find their domestic employees through the American embassy newsletter, *La Palabre*. Francophone Canadian, European, and Middle Eastern aid workers typically use the Facebook group Super Mamans de Dakar, a general group for mostly expat mothers in Dakar, or Dakarium, a more targeted Facebook group for hiring and advertising domestic employees, which uses both French and English and is populated by middle-class and elite Senegalese as well as expats. Though domestic workers sometimes advertise themselves in all three of these spaces, it is generally departing employers who recommend their current workers for hire.

The ads on these sites differ in length and emphasis. *La Palabre* is notable for the length and detail of its ads. The recommendations are often impassioned, reflecting the anxiety of employers to acquit themselves of the duty of finding a new position for their domestic worker before they leave. Originally a paper newsletter, now online, *La Palabre* has a section called "Classifieds: Domestic Help," where expats advertise for their current and former domestic employees, usually just before or after leaving the country and leaving them unemployed.

The ads reveal many of the underlying assumptions and desires of employers, as well as what they are willing to admit in the way of expectations, thereby giving "insight into how reasonable employers consider these expectations to be" (Lair, MacLeod, and Budgar 2016, 287). I analyzed all the ads in *La Palabre* from 2014 to 2017 to get a sense of what kinds of qualities expat employers assume hiring expats are looking for. Though there is certainly some difference between what American expats seek from a domestic worker and, for example, what French or Indian employers in Senegal desire from their workers, this analysis still illuminates many general trends across cultures. Each job has key words, phrases, and qualities that recur as selling points for that position—what the poster imagines will be appealing to an audience of potential new employers. These selected qualities reveal not only what are desired qualities for domestic employees but also what are assumed to be hard-to-find, distinguishing characteristics that set the employee apart from others. In what follows I offer a real ad from the newsletter as an example,[4] then detail job-specific qualities found across the ads I analyzed. As these jobs are generally quite gendered (gardeners/drivers/security guards = male; nannies/housekeepers/cooks = female), some of these qualities and key phases are gendered as well.

Gardeners/Drivers/Guards

HARD WORKING GARDENER: MALIQ SIDIBE

Gardener: Maliq Sidibe

I have had the pleasure of working with the most hard working individual in Senegal! Maliq has been my gardener since we arrived
two years ago. Without exaggeration, I truly have never had an employee work so hard and regularly as Maliq. He has only missed
three days of work in the two years and that was to nurse malaria.
He loves his craft, takes meticulous care of my garden and keeps my
bougainvilliers flowering all year! The ficus is huge and my patio
area is always meticulous. He works four mornings/week for me.
He shows up spot on by 7:30 a.m. and works hard until he finishes.
He charges an initial "clean up fee" and then takes his monthly
salary. He purchases the necessary pesticides to keep the white
flies from killing everything and some compost once in a while.
He won't ask for money except for these items and always produces
a receipt. He has been a wonderful part of our team, always has a
smile and is truly the hardest working person I've hired! He works
for other embassy families and is RSO vetted.[5] You can reach him
at [redacted]. Feel free to contact me as well at [redacted].

Posted on January 12, 2015

For the jobs that skew male, three categories of key words appeared
and reappeared in the classifieds recommending particular men for
these positions. The first category was assertions about the men's
honesty and trustworthiness, usually emphasized with superlatives
or illustrated through particular acts of honesty: "Above all he is
extraordinarily honest"; "very honest"; "scrupulously honest"; "will
work for your best interest when negotiating prices in the markets and
plant nurseries, and he always brings back the change." The second
category was a declaration that the gardener/guard/driver was a hard
worker who could be relied on to show and up and take his work seriously: "a fabulous work ethic"; "extraordinarily devoted"; "completely

reliable"; "only missing days when he was sick and almost always after coming to our house as scheduled to tell us that he was not feeling well." The third category was more nebulous character traits, seemingly unconnected to the performance of the work (need a gardener be humble?) but making for enjoyable relations with the employee: "a very respectful demeanor"; "polite"; "humble"; "helpful"; "courteous and pleasant personality"; "quiet and humble"; "extremely communicative, thoughtful, and conscientious."

These ads show how flexible and multifaceted the jobs turn out to be. As is common in informal domestic work, the job usually expands to things way outside the normal job description associated with the title (Grover 2018). A gardener's ad said, "Besides gardening he will run errands, sweep and wash down patios and do windows." Another gardener "also takes great care of the car, washing it regularly inside and out." An ad for a combination of gardener/dog caretaker listed even more varied duties: "He also does other things like cleaning up the garage, sofas, hanging pictures, does other errands without complaining." One ad for a security guard said that his employers call upon him for additional skills that fall far outside the usual job description, noting proudly: "We have also trusted Abdoulaye to serve as a cultural interpreter for our guests." A gardener who "sweeps and cleans our driveway" was touted as "also an excellent pet-handler." The ad detailed the myriad pet-related activities the gardener was responsible for: "He takes our dog for a walk every day, washes him once a week, and plays with him in the garden while we are at work. He also takes care of our dog and cat while we are on leave."

Pet care was listed frequently as a duty of gardeners, security guards, and drivers. Authors of ads noted when their employee not only took on the maintenance and care for pets but seemed to become emotionally attached to them as well:[6] "Étienne took our dogs for walks in the mornings around our neighborhood and showed genuine care for their well-being." "Our dogs adore him," one ad claimed. Security guards, gardeners, and drivers who put in emotional labor were rewarded with claims like "very good with the dogs and seemed to enjoy them"; "lovingly looking after our pets"; "spoils our dog." Two of the ads were accompanied photos of smiling Senegalese men in an outdoor green space holding dogs.

Some ads underlined the importance of a male employee's emotional connection and relation to other household members, especially the employer's children. One ad said a driver "handles children well"; another said a male errand boy "enjoys children." A security guard was praised for winning the approval of the children: "Our children absolutely adore him and loved to talk with him or try to help him with his work. He is so patient and kind with them and was even up for a little soccer practice with our son if time allowed." A sports connection was also noted in another ad: "He is also caring, great with kids (plays soccer with our boys)."

Often ads emphasized the amount of experience an advertised employee has had working for other expats: "Sow has been with us for almost 2 years, but has been employed by embassy personnel since 2001. Along with our recommendation, he has a stack of letters of recommendations from his previous work as both a day guard and gardener." "Note that Claude worked for 12 years at the Club Atlantic (formerly Club American), and knows Americans and other expats well." Experience with expatriates and their ways were a confirmation of trustworthiness and quality of work.

The highest form of praise was reserved for employees who barely felt like employees at all. "We really can't say enough great things about this man who is more like a family member than a staff member."

Housekeepers/Nannies/Cooks

DOMESTIC HELP: HOUSEKEEPER—ELOÏSE GUEYE

Eloïse is one of the best housekeepers that our family has ever had. She is extremely hard-working, calm, friendly and 100 percent trustworthy. She began working for us in March 2016. In a very short time, she mastered her responsibilities in keeping our house neat and clean. She works with very little direction and always shows initiative. She keeps the kitchen organized and does laundry well including ironing. It is wonderful to come home every day to a spotless house! This is what we hired her to do, and she does it very well. She is also friendly, humble, open-minded and takes specific direction from us without complaint and always follows through. She also has good judgement and knows when to come to us for "approval" before doing something a bit out of the norm. An absolutely sweet and loving person, the bonus with Eloïse is that she's wonderful with our son who fell in love with her. While her primary responsibility is housekeeping duties, she does an excellent job in caring for our 9-year-old son. She meets him at the bus stop, takes him on play dates, and ensures that he is on time for his extracurricular activities. She is very loving and caring with our son so we have no hesitation to leave him in her hands. While I do most of the cooking, Eloise assists in the preparation of food and she makes delicious Yassa poulet (local food) as well as some Asian dishes. She is willing to learn new dishes and she is a quick learner. Eloïse is always on time and has often come on a weekend day to lend an extra hand. We are extremely satisfied with her work and have never had a single issue. Eloïse speaks fluent French and Wolof. She knows just a few words of English but she is trying to learn more. We feel extremely lucky to have found her. We are leaving post in December and we hope she finds a spot in another family where she feels as appreciated and brings as much joy as she has to our home. You can contact Eloïse directly at [redacted]. Feel free to contact me ([redacted]) directly for a reference at [redacted]. You can also contact me with questions at [redacted].

Posted on October 24, 2017

The ads for female-gendered work had some of the same themes as those for male-gendered work. Employers touted their nannies' and housekeepers' honesty and trustworthiness, with phrases like "very honest" and "honest to a fault." A few gave examples that showed that a lack of honesty means a concern that money would be taken or misappropriated, stressing that their housekeeper "keeps meticulous records of money"; "she would do the grocery shopping off a list, and would provide a detailed accounting of costs and always return with any leftover money provided." Anecdotes such as "there were several times she found money in our laundry pockets and returned it" matched anecdotes about finding and returning money that came up quite a bit in my interviews (see chapter 2).

In addition to emphasizing their honesty, employers declared their employees-for-hire to be "dependable" and "reliable." Many asserted this through lauding their employees' complete availability and their failure to take any personal leave. "She is very dependable and has not missed a day in her two years of employment," one said. Employers saw their employees' dedication to their work above their own personal health and family needs as a selling point. "During her employment with us, I have had to insist on her taking time off due to a death in her family," one ad mentioned, while another boasted, "Evangeline has worked for me for a year—5 days a week, and has never called in sick." A lack of any other priorities or boundaries made for an attractive domestic worker: "Marie has never been late or called in sick (she starts at 7:30 a.m.) and she will work late into the evening when I ask her to. I have never had a problem with changing her schedule around or having her come on a Saturday as needed." "She made herself available on evenings and weekends whenever we needed her."

Ads praised housekeepers' hard work, saying maids were "thorough," "meticulous," "hardworking," and had a "strong work ethic" and promoted their skills in cleaning and tidying. A few praised "military style bed making" and the ability to iron a man's shirt to even a fussy husband's satisfaction. Several emphasized their house's "sparkling" cleanliness thanks to their worker: "The house is squeaky clean by the time she's done for the day" and "Our home is spotless, cared for and comfortable because of Anta."

Descriptions of the kind of cooking the housekeeper could do were the most detailed parts of these ads from expats for expats. People far from home want the comfort of familiar foods, and many domestic workers of expats have learned a wide range of cuisines to cater to them. "We love her cooking—she has a large repertoire of meals and cooks American/European, Ivorian, and Senegalese dishes for us," one ad promised. Another ad from someone who had already left their post in Senegal waxed nostalgic, saying, "Maimouna's cooking is something I miss everyday! From her crepes and oatmeal, to all her Senegalese dishes (thiebujen, yassa, thiou, mafe, couscous, les grillades), to some French and American favorites (baked chicken, quiche, veggies in a béchamel sauce, spaghetti, French fries), her cakes, and her great juices, which she kept the freezer stocked with (bissap, ginger, ditax)." Many ads listed specific dishes in this way ("makes terrific marinara sauce, lasagna, and banana bread"), while other emphasized the housekeeper's ability to cater to the specific tastes of her employers ("she always ensured a fresh salad was available for me"; "she can make toubab-y versions[7] of several Senegalese dishes"). By far, the most common refrain about cooking in these ads was how quick and adept the domestic workers were at learning to make whatever the employers desired. Several different ads mentioned the same refrain: "If you show her a recipe once, she is quick to repeat without help!" "If you find a recipe that you would like her to cook, all you need to supply is the ingredients and directions"; "I sometimes just print something off the internet and review it with her, and she'll make it!" Some mentioned that maids could read from French cookbooks, and one claimed the maid could read recipes in English as well. One ad touted the fact that the maid was Christian and thus "will buy and cook pork dishes if you'd like." Another said that the housekeeper taught her employer to cook a few Senegalese dishes as well.

Next to cooking, the most detail was given in descriptions of how nannies cared for kids and how "great with children" or "amazing with children" they were. Many of the ads emphasized the kind of emotional labor nannies performed: "Her love and care of our son is something rarely seen anywhere in the world, but, perhaps, from a mother herself" ; "She cares for our son as though he were her own." This is a familiar aspect of the commodification of love that researchers of care workers have analyzed.[8] Many ads mentioned the child's love for the nanny as well, how she was part of the family, and how much the children would or did miss her.

In addition to love, however, ads praised nannies for their ability to discipline. "She knows when to say 'no' when necessary," said one. The fact that the nanny was firm was often paired with the words *kind* and *nurturing*, suggesting that this balance was ideal. The word *vigilant* was used to advertise several nannies—in one case for attentiveness to the daughter's food allergies, but generally in the ability to be the eyes of the employer when the employer was working. Several went into detail about the scrupulous vigilance and reporting back that their employee performed: "She is very diligent to let you know if anything unusual happened during the day, if the child got hurt, or if she noticed any potential health issue." "She keeps a notebook where she gives a daily detailed account of his day, including his eating habits, play, and any special moments we may have missed. She often includes pictures!" Others emphasized their trust in their nanny to care for the children while the parents were out of town, *en mission*: "She is good with technology and was able to ensure that I could skype my son while travelling."

Examples of a nanny's specialized skills were detailed ("she bakes muffins, makes chicken nuggets from scratch, and reads to our son every day") as were the specific tasks her job included: "She was able to handle our two kids, whether for routine homework, meals, naps, bathing, free play, or for excursions to the zoo, the trampoline, Sea Plaza.[9]" I noticed an emphasis on educational play; employers offered examples that gave credit to their nannies as educators. "She doesn't just watch over children, but talks constantly to our little guy, engages him in age-appropriate play, draws and paints with him, and has worked with him on colors, shapes, numbers, and letters in French. I'm convinced that she's responsible for a good deal of his language development!" "Our son has mini-lessons where she has taught him his numbers, shapes, letters, and colors. She also gives him lessons in French language. They paint, plant seeds, and sing songs." Moreover, they framed this as something the nanny loved to do, something that was a pleasurable and recreational part of her work: "She loves to play with the kids, interacting with them with singing, playing games, and teaching them their colors, numbers, animals (in English and French!)." "She also can play. I believe she has become an excellent Lego creator!"

As do their male counterparts, female domestic employees perform a wide range of tasks truly earning the French expression *bonne à tout faire*. The range is discernable though the various specific tasks mentioned in the ads. Keeping the house clean included making beds, tidying, general cleaning, cleaning kitchens and bathrooms, dusting, vacuuming, polishing furniture, and doing laundry but also "identifying and doing seasonal or occasional tasks such as shampooing carpets, washing windows, cleaning the distiller, defrosting the freezers, washing the kids' sneakers, organizing closets" in one case. In another, the employee "arranged for my furniture to be re-upholstered for very cheap (pickup and delivery)." Housekeepers "help unpack and organize our shipment," meaning the furniture and belongings shipped from overseas. Another perk: "If you travel, she will adapt her vacation dates to you and will set up the house and shop for food and even cook for your arrival." Niche skills like "soap making, bissap wine making and dress making" were listed as perks in employing a particular housekeeper. One helpful housekeeper "calls plumbers, carpenters, electricians, veterinarians" whenever she observed a problem. Another "will fix buttons that have fallen off without asking, remove stains from everything."

Employers praised their employees-for-hire for being *proactive*. This word reoccurred many times, as did the phrase *takes initiative*.

One noted appreciatively, "I always thought she had a great deal of common sense." This praise connected to other personal qualities that were touted in these ads like humility, integrity, pride in work, and professionalism. One ad noted the housekeeper was "respectful of authority"; another said the employee was "clean" and "presents herself well," but most ads focused more on the kindness and pleasantness of the company of this stranger in the home. *Warm* was a word that many used to describe their nanny or housekeeper. *Sunny* and *always cheerful* were also used. One ad included this assessment: "She is a pleasure to be around—we discussed many things over the years about culture, politics, raising kids, and life in general. I have much respect for her as a person, not to mention as an employee." Another said she had a "a wonderful disposition"; a second, "a soft and loving demeanor"; and another concluded that her housekeeper's "energy, enthusiasm for the job, and positive attitude are unmatched. . . . She was a pleasure to have around our house."

A key selling feature for a nanny or a housekeeper was simply that this was not her first rodeo. A domestic employee who had worked for other expat families, but especially for other American families was highly valued by the readers and advertisers of *La Palabre*. One ad stated flatly, "We hired Marie because of her impressive 18-year job history working for American families." "She has been working with [expat/American] families for over X years" was a refrain in most of the ads. Ads noted that the nanny or maid could provide letters of recommendations from previous US employers as well. One ad noted that the nanny "was trained in cooking, cleaning, hygiene, and child care by American missionaries in Guinea." Simple experience with other Americans represented a key qualification because it promised some degree of vetting by "people like us," as well as a foundation of shared understanding that eliminated the need for the exhausting and potentially awkward task of explaining how "we" do things. A security guard who already knows that he needs to pick up after the dog, a maid who won't put cashmere sweaters into the dryer, and a nanny who understands the importance of healthy snacks and educational games for the kids are prizes indeed.

DESIRABLE CHARACTERISTICS

Two characteristics did not come through in the ads and yet were somehow omnipresent among the domestic workers that employers had hired. A disproportionate number of expat aid workers I interviewed had nannies or maids who were of the Diola ethnicity or Catholic, or both. Of the five dominant ethnic groups (Wolof, Pulaar, Serer, Diola, and Mandingue), the Diolas represent only about 5 percent of the population. Few of the expat aid workers had noticed the prevalence of Diolas among expat domestic staff—indeed, it was often I who informed them that their employees were from the Casamance (where the majority of ethnic Diola come from), which was evident to me from their last names.

A 2015 survey of maids for Senegalese families in Dakar also found Diola and Christian women to be overrepresented relative to their overall proportion in the population (Ndari 2018, 38),[10] though not nearly in the same proportions as their overrepresentation among expat households. There is a long history of female Diola migration to Dakar (Foucher 2005). Diola (and Serer) women are more likely to engage in urban migration than their counterparts in other ethnicities.[11] Chain migration and the kind of informal recommendation system outlined above account for some aspects of the strong presence of Diola migrants in the population of domestic workers in Dakar.

Although not one expat in an interview said that they purposely sought out a domestic worker from the Casamance or of the Diola ethnicity, there was something more to this preponderance. One blog post from an expat blogger in 2014 spelled out "the scoop" on house help in Senegal for expat newcomers who might not be familiar with the dynamics of finding and managing domestic workers, saying flatly: "The best house helpers are Diola from the Casamance." An expat employee of a religious development organization posted in the comments, "Definitely Diola!" When another commenter wrote disapprovingly that "the ethnic branding is not very helpful and actually harmful" and might discourage expats from hiring a qualified applicant of another ethnicity, the blogger replied cheerfully that she was quoting Senegalese domestic workers who spoke in terms of ethnicity, and she added, "My house helper is not Diola, btw. And she's wonderful!"

The reason that expats specifically hire such large numbers of Diola housekeepers may have to do with the other characteristic that is rarely advertised but disproportionately present among the housekeepers and nannies of expats: Christianity. Over half the domestic workers of expats I interviewed were Catholic, and well over half the expats who I interviewed had Catholic maids or nannies. This is particularly striking, as Senegal is approximately 95 percent Muslim, with Catholics making up only about 4 percent of the population. Most of Senegal's Catholics are of Diola ethnicity or are Serer, the other overrepresented ethnic group among migrant domestic workers in Dakar (Hesseling 1985, 88), so these two facts are likely linked.

The links between Catholicism and domestic work are not incidental. Les Sœurs du Bon Pasteur, an order of nuns with a strong social service presence in Senegal, have, in addition to orphanages and women's shelters, a vocational school that trains young Catholic women to be domestic workers.[12] The Maria Goretti Training Center[13] offers instruction in childcare, cooking, home economics, and housework. The trainees apply what they learn, working with children in the nearby orphanage and daycare run by the nuns. The training center helps them find positions as domestic workers, starting them as "interns" in homes of church members. The domestic workers I interviewed who had gone through the program said that they also used contacts with other young women they had met during their training to help them find jobs. The program costs less than $100 a year and includes housing and meals during the week. The tuition of many of the girls is paid by scholarships from Catholic donors around the world.

One of the domestic workers I interviewed, Rose, did two years of training with the nuns. She had moved to Dakar from the Casamance to live with her aunt and attend school. Upon dropping out of high school, she found her aunt couldn't support her to the extent she required, so she decided to find her own source of income. After Rose completed the Marie Goretti training program, she was placed in her "internship" in the home of a Spanish foreign service family in Dakar. She ended up being hired full-time by the family as the live-in maid and nanny and worked there for five years until she got married and became pregnant. Now, Rose balances motherhood with her job as the housekeeper and cook for an American employee of the Peace Corps.

I asked Rose if she had any insights into why it was so common for expats to hire Catholic maids and nannies. She paused from scrubbing a large cooking pot in the sink of her employer's kitchen and thought for a moment. Rose said there are some expats who prefer a girl who was trained by the nuns, because if there are problems, they can send her back to the nuns. She knew this was a possibility during her employment with the Spanish family she interned for and said she tried hard to stay in their good graces so that wouldn't happen. Not all Catholic maids and nannies were trained by nuns, she noted as she picked up the pot and went back to scrubbing, but still there were toubabs who just prefer a Catholic maid. "It's just a preference" she said.

There are several reasons why expat aid workers would specifically seek out a Catholic housekeeper, cook, or nanny. Raised in the Catholic Church and in Catholic schools, their mastery of written and spoken French might be superior to that of Muslim rural migrants who have attended Koranic schools or received primary instruction in indigenous languages.[14] The command of French is particularly important to francophone expats, but non-francophone expats also find it easier to communicate with house staff in French, as few expat development workers have had training in local languages. An aid worker for a Catholic development organization said that it made sense that her organization hired many Catholics, but noted that many Senegalese hired at embassies and development organizations were also Catholic. She attributed this preference to Catholic schooling, which many non-Catholics in Senegal also feel is superior.[15]

One French aid worker expressed something akin to discomfort with Muslims in her home, though she disavowed that explanation. When a potential nanny came to be interviewed, Sylvie was surprised that she was wearing a veil. Though most of the Senegalese population is Muslim, women are seldom veiled, with the exception of those belonging to more strict conservative sects, such as the Ibadou.[16] "Now, that doesn't necessarily trouble me," she insisted, "but afterwards she was imposing all the conditions and that bothered me. For example, she wouldn't cook pork. So I said to myself, 'Look, already starting with these little things, this risks becoming more complicated.'" Sylvie eventually hired a Catholic nanny, a Maria Goretti Training Center classmate of a friend's nanny.

A few other expat aid workers echoed this idea that it was important to have a domestic employee who would cook and handle pork. Others wanted a nanny who would take the Christian holidays off, and not the Muslim holidays, because this would be more convenient for their own holiday schedules. Several intentionally hired both a Catholic and a Muslim domestic worker, thus ensuring that both sets of holidays would be covered. Alain, a single man who works at a French NGO focused on food security and famine, told me that although he did not go looking for a Catholic housekeeper, he was glad that his "nanny for grown-ups" as he refers to her, Pascaline, can drink a glass of wine with him after work, something that would be unthinkable had she been Muslim.

SALARY

An additional element that was rarely mentioned in these ads was salary. This mirrors the reluctance of many aid workers to bluntly tell one another (or nosey anthropologists) the exact figure they pay their domestic employees, lest it be thought too little or too much. Only two of the classified ads I reviewed discussed it at all. In one ad, "**reasonable salary**" was a standalone perk, presumably signaling that the housekeeper did not require an overly inflated wage; another ad informed potential new bosses that "because she did all," they had paid their domestic worker "200,000 CFA/month" (roughly $350), at the upper end of the norm for expats.

It is a truth universally acknowledged that expat bosses pay more than local ones for their domestic care. All my interviewees—aid workers and domestic workers alike—noted this substantial pay difference. According to my interviews and other sources, maids for Senegalese families in Dakar generally earn about 35,000 CFA francs ($60) per month,[17] substantially below what is the minimum wage in Senegal (the SMIG, or Guaranteed Minimum Interprofessional Salary, which is currently about 300 CFA francs per hour).

For expats, finding out what to pay their domestic staff can be a bit mysterious. Aid worker interviewees were eager to ask me how what they paid compared to others I had spoken to. Every once in a while, someone new to town will post a general question about housekeeper or nanny salaries on one of the Dakar expat social media groups, and it always creates a bit of tension in the response as people argue for and against different salary scales and righteously justify their own idea of a fair salary. An expat blog run by an American woman active in the expat community in Dakar acknowledged the mystery surrounding best practices and tried to clear it up. In 2014, she interviewed a few domestic workers with experience working for expats and asked them for their input. Curiously, she put salary in terms of a daily rate, whereas all my aid worker and domestic worker interviewees spoke in terms of a monthly salary. She stated, "The going daily rate for house helpers (and nannies and cooks) working for expats in Dakar is between 4,000–5,000 CFA, but those with many years of experience and training can make up to 7,500 CFA. This is well above the minimum wage, which is 209 CFA/hour." She notes that a daily transportation allowance of 500–1,000 CFA francs per day might also be applied. The standard is also to give one month of paid vacation after a year of employment, called "the thirteenth month"—though this is often taken as an extra month of pay rather than a month off work.

Among my interviewees, I found that the average monthly wage for a full-time domestic worker seemed to be about 120,000 CFA a month (roughly $200) for a nanny or housekeeper, with an average of 10 hours per day of work, five or six days a week, though the hours and responsibilities differed widely depending on the family. Even with the inflations of the urban, expat domestic labor market, the salaries of domestic workers are still quite low relative to the compensation that development workers receive, and unthinkably low compared to what such labor would cost in the United States, where, for example, the federal minimum wage has been (an outrageously low) $7.25 an hour since 2009.

In most interviews, aid workers said they had "asked around"—spoken to colleagues and other expats—about how much to pay for what hours and services, and then discussed with their potential employee until they agreed on a price. Jillian, a faith-based INGO employee, said that she took her domestic employees' previous salaries as a point of reference for setting their wage. She negotiated with her nanny and her housekeeper by first asking what they had made in their previous jobs. "So actually, one, she was being paid what seemed to be quite well and she had just gotten a raise at the end of her time. So she seemed to want to be okay with being lower but we were like, 'No, we'll keep you there.' And then the other lady, she was only part time and we had her go full time for us so we basically doubled what she had been making before."

"Awkward" was a word many aid workers used when describing this negotiation over salary, where they held competing desires to be fair, charitable, and savvy enough not to get swindled. Lori, a USAID employee, described what she called the "awkward salary negotiation" thusly: "You know there's that whole thing, the person says something, and you're like 'No! I couldn't possibly pay $100!' And you're like, 'Yeah, you could.' But there's no base to go off of unless the previous person has told you how much, and in which case you should go up a little bit. Because I would, if I went to a new job."

Lori was pleased and impressed that Hortense, whom she eventually hired as a part-time housekeeper, came ready with letters of recommendation from previous employers that disclosed her salary with them. Though Hortense's responsibilities were much fewer for Lori and her husband compared to the much larger household she ran for her previous employer, Lori appreciated her initiative and agreed to pay her at the same rate. Hortense had worked for several expat families before Lori and her husband and was, as Lori put it, "very direct" about the terms of employment, insisting on a formal contract that spelled out her days off, allowances for transport, and her prorated thirteenth month.

Not all domestic workers are as direct or as organized as Hortense in their salary negotiations. Many domestic workers I spoke to also found the process awkward, not wanting to harm their chances of being hired for a desirable job by appearing too demanding at the outset but also not wanting to undervalue their labor when noncommittal expat employers were trying to defer to their expectations.

Diariatou, for example, had never worked for expats before she was hired by aid workers Alice and Marco. Alice and Marco had just arrived in Dakar and thus they felt a bit tentative about the norms and what represented a fair wage. As Diariatou recalled, she and her potential employers were feeling each other out, each reluctant to make an inappropriate or disadvantageous first offer. She recounted, "They said, 'What's your price?' Me, as I'd never worked before, I said, 'Well, what do you propose?'" Eventually, after Alice surveyed her expat aid worker colleagues, they settled on 80,000 CFA francs for Diariatou to come three days a week, clean the house, care for the cat, and do some light cooking. Alice assessed the amount she paid Diariatou as "pretty decent," calculating that the workload was especially light because she and her husband had no kids. "I've heard of people paying ridiculously low amounts, which I think is really shameful," Alice told me.

The majority of my expat interviewees spoke with evident concern about paying fair wages for the work, though this conception of "fair" was relative to the local economy, not relative to their own compensation or their home country's conception of a living wage. They often demonstrated this concern for fairness by expressing disapproval of how much other expats paid their workers. Rayna, who works for USAID, declared vaguely that "people are very demanding, and they don't pay, and they come home late." Samantha, who had started a small NGO in Dakar after moving there from France, heard from her housekeeper that some expat families were offering local rates. "They've talked to their Senegalese neighbors and find out their Senegalese neighbors are paying 35,000." Samantha scoffed at the audacity of these expats who would try to pay only local rates, then confided, "My friend and I have this really tacky WhatsApp chat going at all times where we screenshot ridiculous posts by expats, like 'I want this person to raise my children, cook my meals' and then they want to pay like 80,000. I'm like, 'You want to go lie on the beach all day while someone else lives your life!'"

Alma, the country director of a faith-based INGO recounted a day when a new colleague asked other expats in her office for advice about how much to pay her house help. "I was really shocked," Alma recalled, recounting how her colleagues responded. "There was someone paying 50,000," about $85 a month for a full-time nanny and maid. "And there was another one paying 90,000 CFA." When Alma and a couple of other colleagues shared that they were paying much more—closer to $250 a month—the two colleagues who were paying very little reacted not with embarrassment but with indignation. "They were outraged that we were paying too much. And I was like, 'Really?' That thing, it really surprised me, because it's like, 'You make a really good salary.'"

A few of my interviewees expressed surprise that fellow aid workers wouldn't see fair pay as a value in line with their own careers as development workers. For Jillian, like Alma, salary negotiation was a matter of justice: "Even if the market is lower, why should I be cheap about it when they're providing—yeah—this great care, but also, it doesn't seem really just to me. Nickel and diming someone, I mean."

Not everyone was certain that fair pay meant high pay. Kim, a French-American aid worker, told me frankly, "I think Americans overpay." She laughed and continued, "And my view on that is, look, try to get what you think is reasonable and what they accept. They, I don't think they would accept something they didn't . . ." She trails off and then recounts that her own maid pushed back against her initial offer because it was too low and together they found an amount they could agree upon.

Gemma too, was candid about not wanting to overpay. She hired a housekeeper who had worked for her American friends in the south of Senegal, despite some misgivings, because she was a good deal. "She wasn't perfect, but she was a lot cheaper because I think she hadn't worked for Americans in Dakar." Dakar's domestic worker salaries are higher than in other parts of Senegal, which have lower cost of living and fewer expats to create a separate expat economy. Even though her housekeeper's former employers were expats, they likely paid a salary more in line with what their southern Senegalese neighbors paid, thus giving Gemma's housekeeper different expectations about salary. Though her housing, twenty-four-hour guard service, and the school fees for her two children at the expensive International School of Dakar were paid for by her employer, Gemma was eager to capitalize on these low expectations and pay her housekeeper below the expat market rate for the reproductive labor that allowed Gemma to advance in her career in poverty reduction without sacrificing her family life.

CONDITIONS OF LABOR

In the main, both aid workers and their domestic workers assert that expat salaries are superior to what local families pay, and most insist that the work conditions are also better. Stories about Senegalese bosses and the potential horrors of working for them populate my interviews with domestic workers working for expat bosses. Some of my interviewees had firsthand experience working for Senegalese families before they ended up in the circuit of expat households. Others had friends or family employed by Senegalese bosses. Diariatou, who hailed from the Casamance region of Senegal, for instance, told me of a friend who worked for a Senegalese family. "Take my one friend," Diariatou began, in the midst of a conversation comparing expats to Senegalese as bosses, "30,000 they paid her. She has two kids, she has to pay rent, she has to work Sundays, has no day off, no holidays." Working seven days a week, twelve months a year, is not uncommon among domestic workers for Senegalese families, though Senegalese labor law requires one day off a week and a paid month of holiday each year. Because of the informal nature of the work, it is largely unregulated and labor abuses abound. Workers are sometimes let go without pay for real or imagined infractions such as laziness, theft, or even a single day of absence (Diaw 1996, 274; Diome 2013, 4).

Diariatou had worked in Senegalese households as well when she had first arrived in Dakar as a young woman. "Where I worked, it was hard and they don't give you respect," she said simply. She added that there had been no health insurance, but it wouldn't have mattered, because there were no sick days. "You work yourself sick and they don't heal you. You work until they let you go. Sometimes before you get home, it's dusk." She described the lack of dignity afforded by the job: "It's as though you aren't a person."

Others interviewees had been required to stay the night with their employers, basically being on-call full time. A frequent line in ads for nannies or maids in posts by Senegalese employers on sites like Dakarium is "descendre tous les samedis," meaning that the employee will return to her home only Saturday nights for her day of rest and return to live-in work the following night. Also common is the phrase "quinzaine" or "descendre tous les 15 jours" meaning that the worker will get every second Sunday off.[18] A study by the NGO Enda Tiers Monde found that two-thirds of young domestic workers in Dakar lived with their employers (Diaw 1996, 272). The lack of formal contracts or oversight in almost all contexts of domestic work in Senegal means that there are few constraints on what employers can demand from their workers.

The International Labour Organization (ILO) characterizes domestic labor as one of the most problematic sectors of labor, not only because of difficult work conditions but also because of the prevalence of physical, psychological, and sexual violence (D'Souza 2010). This kind of abuse exists alongside the more mundane kinds of exploitation like no sick days, no vacation days, sleeping over, working tirelessly with ever-expanding responsibilities. In other contexts, excessively long hours, low pay, and unreasonable workload expectations have been shown to be commonplace for domestic work.[19]

In Dakar, a supply that outweighs demand gives local employers a great deal of power in negotiating low wages and grueling hours (Gassama 2005, 171), not to mention impunity in other forms of exploitation and abuse.[20] That these young women are typically migrants and thus distanced from their families subjects them to further vulnerability. Low salaries combined with domestic workers usually being young, rural migrant women with low levels of education means that they tend to have precarious housing arrangements and be at higher risk for various health problems as well as being tempted to enter riskier, more lucrative professions like sex work (Ndari 2018, 61). They access very little social protection from the state, despite Senegal having laws against the exploitation of vulnerable populations, having signed international conventions such as UN Convention 189 on domestic workers, and having numerous government institutions and NGOs that should protect the rights of internal migrants.[21]

Globally, there have been movements to formalize and unionize domestic workers.[22] Yet the invisibility of domestic labor, tucked away in the private space of the home, makes it much harder to regulate. Additionally, the lack of a common boss to target makes enforcement of rights and norms challenging. Furthermore, domestic workers themselves often do not consider that they are doing "real work" or are professionals who are entitled to labor protections. Domestic service is informal whether for Senegalese families or expat families; thus domestic workers generally don't harbor expectations of unionization or state protection. This is compounded in Senegal by domestic workers' general lack of formal education and mastery of the juridical language of Senegal, French. Thus, very few domestic workers attempt to seek justice or protection from exploitation through the judicial system.

One recourse domestic workers do have is their ability to leave work. With no formal contract and bad conditions, domestic workers often opt to leave their post when they are treated badly, when they find better pay or better conditions elsewhere, or when they simply wish to return home to their village (Gassama 2005, 171). Turnover in domestic work is extremely high, and Senegalese families complain constantly about how hard it is to find and keep good help, though they remain unwilling to pay more for the labor.

In Senegal, conditions for domestic workers are starting to improve, but not by much. The Centre d'écoute des jeunes filles domestiques, a professionalization school for domestic workers, was created in 2011 and has been graduating small classes of young women with not only employable skills but a basic understanding of Senegalese labor law and the rights of domestic workers. The NGO Enda Tiers Monde has created an association of household employees to protect the moral and material rights of domestic workers, yet there are few members, and very few eligible workers are aware of the association or its actions (Bop 2010, 5).

CONTRACTS AND DUTIES

Across the world, domestic work is largely informal work and often takes place without a formal contract between employer and employee. Burnham and Theodore note that employers of domestic workers have an unusual amount of power over employees and the labor process, including "the power to hire and fire, to determine the scope and the conditions of work, to set wages, and to provide or withhold benefits" (2012, 8).[23]

Though it is quite unusual for Senegalese employers to have a contract with their domestic workers, expats are slightly more likely to use them (Diaw 1996, 273). A few of the aid workers I interviewed had signed formal contracts with members of their domestic staff. Workers for USAID had to follow a relatively new rule to register their domestic workers and their contracts with them with the US embassy; the embassy provided a sample contract for its employees to use.[24] Lori believed the rule was instituted because of accusations of misconduct on the part of American employers by domestic workers: "People were coming to the embassy after that person had left and saying, 'You owe me money. This person left and they owed me money and they didn't pay it.' Especially around the severance issue. Because you have to pay them severance and it has to be in the contract."

Lori used the sample contract but amended it to her housekeeper's wishes in certain ways. For example, the sample contract has employers paying quarterly taxes on behalf of the maid, because employers are legally obliged to pay into social security and pension funds in Senegal. Few house staff wanted this money taken out of their salary and sent into a social security program that they didn't expect would benefit them in the future. To get around this, everyone I talked to who had a contract simply paid this money directly to the employee and stipulated in the contract that the employee was responsible for making these payments to the government, which no domestic worker whom I spoke to subsequently did.

Rayna's nannies were uncomfortable with the idea of a formal contract. "I'm like, 'We have to do it. You do what you need to do on your side, I'm not going to tell you how to do it, but on our side we have to.'" Like Lori, she paid the "taxes" directly to her nannies: "We actually ended up in the process giving them a raise. So it worked out for them. But they were really weirded out about it at first. And I was like, 'This has nothing to do with our relationship or our communication. It has to do with a requirement from the embassy.' It took them a little while and they felt really constricted about it. But I reassured them every time that it shouldn't affect anything." For Rayna, a contract was simply a formality—something required by the bureaucracy of her job, not something she felt had any value to her employees or any possibility of affecting their rights and treatment.

Most aid workers had no obligation to their employer to formalize their contracts with their domestic employees, and so the very idea of a contract never occurred to them. Tamara's faith-based NGO had no such rule, so she took a very casual approach to setting the terms of her arrangement with her nanny: "We didn't have a contract. We didn't sign contracts. I just talked to her—like, 'What do you want?'" Some told me they didn't bother with a contract because they only had a part-time housekeeper so a contract seemed like overkill. Several who worked for USAID told me that no contract was required by the US embassy if it was not full-time employment. In a later interview with an employee of the security office of the US embassy, I found out that this is not in fact the case, but that no follow-up was ever done by the embassy to ensure that staff were adhering to guidelines in their informal hiring. No one that I spoke to had formal contracts with gardeners, guards, or chauffeurs.

Even when formal work contracts were employed, there was usually very little detail in them about the range and scale of duties. As Rayna's comments illustrate, contracts were seen as a bureaucratic formality, not an opportunity to create boundaries or protections in the working relationship. Stipulations of working hours were rarely concrete and changed over time without any update of a contract, and overtime was treated mostly on an ad hoc basis.

Kim's nanny worked from 6:30 a.m. until 7:00 p.m., Monday through Friday and occasionally on Saturdays. Kim insisted to me that these long hours were accidental, as the nanny lived in the outskirts of Dakar and carpooled with a neighbor who had to be in town quite early. The long hours, however, were a blessing to Kim, whose husband was often overseas for his own work. Kim's daughter woke up early and her nanny's early arrival meant Kim could get a bit more sleep before getting up for work by sending her daughter into the nanny's care. "When I hear the door open, I'm like, 'Okay—go have breakfast!' I feel guilty about that though because I should be getting up." Kim said she tried to get home earlier from work, by 6:00 p.m., so that she and her daughter could have the dinner that the nanny made before Kim gave her a bath, read her a book, and put her to bed at 7:30. The nanny usually finished doing the dinner dishes during bath and bedtime, before departing to catch the bus home at 7:00.

Extra hours were treated casually. Kim noted that "if we come back a little late, like 9:00 p.m., we'll give her taxi money, give her a little extra. And when I went away for a work trip and my husband wasn't here, we got her an iPhone and gave her a little extra money because she did a good job. You know, like, she's really good and I want her to be happy." Others said they occasionally paid their full-time employees extra to stay late and "babysit" or to help cook and serve at dinner parties in the evening or on weekends. Several aid workers left their kids with the nanny or maid for the weekend or when they had to travel for work, paying them for the extra time and occasionally inviting the caretaker to bring her children to stay as well.

Figuring out benefits was also complicated for aid workers, with no clear protocol in place. Many development workers compared their management of staff to good or bad management practices that they had experienced in their own careers. Tamara explained that she approached employment of her domestic workers using her employer's practices as a model. "I was like, 'I don't know what to do so I'm going to do the same thing my employer does. You need to go to the doctor? If I get 90 percent of my health insurance covered, I'll pay 90 percent of your visits.'" She also used her previous work experience in setting the terms of the job: "Because I used to work for an hourly wage, I applied everything I knew. You'll get time and a half for overnight, anything during the week. If it's weekend you'll get double." Like Tamara, most approached these kinds of decisions—as well as when to give raises, how to pay severance, and so forth—using their own judgment without any clear rulebook to follow or any accountability to an overseeing body.

In general, the domestic workers I spoke to did not see this informality as problematic. Indeed, few had any expectation that domestic work could be a formal occupation. They were generally cognizant of the fact that, in addition to higher pay, working for expats meant fewer hours and easier working conditions than they could expect from Senegalese employers. Working for expats generally meant using an imported vacuum instead of bending at the waist to sweep in the Senegalese way, and doing laundry with a washer and dryer instead of the brutal-on-the-hands scrubbing by hand in the Senegalese style. Several noted that cooking for expats was also less labor intensive than cooking for Senegalese families. "Their food is so easy to cook," Diariatou said of her American employers. "It is basically just vegetables!"

With expat bosses, both domestic workers and expat employers insisted, working conditions were better. Nevertheless, without protocols for employment and the widespread use of and respect for formal contracts, the labor practices were just as unregulated and the potential for exploitation and labor abuse was still present.

Ironically, the aid workers themselves were often mired in thinking about contracts for their own employment. Many development workers float between short-term and fixed-term positions for part or all of their career, spending time as consultants or trying to be direct hires. They know very well the precarity and insecurity of having to switch employers, of looking for new employment when a project ends, and many talked about their own anxieties on these matters in their interviews. However, aid workers that I spoke to generally had backup plans, had accrued savings and made investments from their work overseas, and were confident that there would be some space within or outside the development industry where they could find another kind of employment at the end of their contract.

When it inevitably came time for them to leave Senegal, they felt some pressure to help their domestic workers find new positions. Many expats did their due diligence of creating an ad or telling their friends, and there were even ads from people who had left years earlier but were still trying to help find placements for their staff. Others felt that all they could do was try, but after they did, it was out of their hands. Rayna, who was preparing to leave her post to return to the US, told her nanny matter-of-factly that when they left Senegal, their obligation to her would end. "I said, 'I can't sponsor you because I don't have the means to sponsor you when I go back.' I can't afford to pay her when I go back."

There is a great deal of talk in the international development industry of creating sustainable livelihoods. This is one of the key phases of the new global development goals—the Sustainable Development Goals. To what extent do the endless arrivals and departures of expat development workers create sustainable livelihoods for those they employ to water their gardens and change their sheets?

When I met her, Madeleine had been working in three separate households at once, spending two days in one, two days in another, and one day a week in the third. By this time a grandmother, Madeleine was worn out and she said the work was too much for her, explaining that in that arrangement, each day she had to clean quite hard because the house had sat uncleaned for days. She eventually convinced one of her employers to hire her full time, but she was nervous the arrangement wouldn't last. As a single man in an apartment who traveled a great deal, her employer did not really need a full-time housekeeper. Madeleine worried that other expats would tell him he was paying too much for too little work. Her employer had recently mentioned a friend who needed a couple of days a week of work, and Madeleine said she was afraid to say no in case her sole boss decided to cut her hours and wages. After decades of working for expat development workers, Madeleine found herself with no real savings, no pension, and no means with which to retire.[25] Her former employers are on to new posts, on to new household staff, ostensibly on a mission to improve the lives of that new country's residents through sustainable social and economic change.

Increasingly, activists and advocates work to bring heretofore invisible domestic work into the discussion of human rights. In 2013, for example, the United Nations Entity for Gender Equality and the Empowerment of Women published a "briefing kit" on implementing protection for domestic workers (UN Women 2013). This briefing kit gives first person narratives from domestic workers around the globe, makes a case for why they should be protected that is designed to appeal to the interests of neoliberal donor governments (domestic workers are productive contributors to economies!), and advocates for extension of labor laws and civil society and government partnerships to support domestic workers.

What this UN document does not do is set out a charter for UN employees to follow in their own employment of domestic workers. There is nary an acknowledgment of the fact that UN employees are employers of domestic laborers themselves—and in fact have been shown to be notoriously exploitative employers of domestic workers. At the sixty-first session of the Commission on Human Rights in 2005, the ACLU and the NGO Global Rights submitted a joint statement entitled "Ending the Exploitation of Migrant Domestic Workers Employed by UN Diplomats and Staff." This statement accuses the UN of failing to hold its employees accountable for violations of the very international human rights and labor laws it drafts and promotes. These range from the denial of basic employment rights, including paying the minimum wage and compensating overtime work, to more extreme kinds of exploitation, including physical, sexual and verbal abuse, detention, and forced labor. In many cases, the statement alleges, the UN employees were protected from criminal prosecution because of their diplomatic status and in fact were transferred to a new position in a different country to avoid being charged for their crimes.

Since this time, although the UN has been very vocal about promoting awareness of the rights of domestic workers in general and in specific countries, it has not turned its attention to its own employees and their treatment of their domestic workers. Currently, no program is in place to monitor the domestic employment practices of UN employees. Though UN employees are encouraged to sign formal contracts with their domestic workers, there is no oversight of this practice nor enforcement of compliance with the stated terms of the contracts. The UN, while championing the rights of domestic workers globally, is reluctant to enforce those rights among its own staff, who see cheap domestic labor as one of the perks and necessities of their job. Broaching the discussion of aid workers and the domestic labor economies they participate in and create is a chief, modest goal of this book. I see it as a continuation of the important advocacy work that others have done to render domestic work more visible.

2 | SECURITY AND
EVERYDAY BORDERING

ERIN AND BRIAN WERE CONCERNED when I told them cheerfully that their building's security guard, Mamadou, had carried my bag upstairs to the third floor for me and into the apartment upon my arrival. They looked at each other uneasily. "We try not to let the guard in the apartment," Erin cautioned me. "Sometimes he hovers by the door and we just thank him and fumble with the keys until he goes downstairs." I felt sheepish and chagrined that I had already made a faux pas, as I was grateful to Erin and Brian for letting me house- and pet-sit in their apartment while they were away. Like many young expat aid workers that I met abroad, they were incredibly generous and welcoming of me, a relative stranger who nonetheless felt instantly familiar. As I noted in the introduction, this was not the first, nor the last time that I house-sat and pet-sat in expat homes in Dakar.

Beyond my embarrassment, I also felt curious. Why was Mamadou not allowed inside the apartment? "It's probably fine," Erin continued after I had apologized. She explained that they don't like when the guards come in because they don't want them knowing exactly what is in the apartment. It wasn't that she necessarily thought their guards would steal, she explained, but she didn't want them discussing what they had seen with other guards on their street or neighbors. "What if they mentioned that we have a big Samsung TV?" she said as an example. "Maybe that would give someone the idea to come and steal it."

They had debated about not giving their housekeeper a key to their apartment for similar reasons and had gone so far as to consult with the neighbor who employed the same housekeeper. When they heard that the other couple did give her a key, they relented and made her one for their apartment so that she could come and clean it when they were at work.

Erin, who is a contractor with a UN agency, and Brian, who works for a private company, chose their third-floor apartment in Dakar's expat-heavy Almadies neighborhood with an eye toward security. They calculated that an apartment that was not on the ground floor or the top floor would be hard to break into from outside. Before they had signed their lease, they walked the perimeter of the building to see if there was any possibility that someone could get in. When they concluded there was not, they signed the papers and moved in.

To have plenty in a context of scarcity is an insecure position. This is the position of most expat aid workers wherever they work. As upper-middle- or middle-class professionals in developing countries who are used to (and often contractually entitled to) Western amenities that are out of reach for the general population, aid workers find themselves feeling various levels of material insecurity, or "moments of unease" (Fechter 2012, 1478). This sense of insecurity, which is enhanced in both formal and informal ways by their employers and peers, shapes their social and domestic lives in particular ways. In this chapter, I explore the role of security in the domestic life of expat aid workers in Senegal. I argue that practices meant to ensure security create distance between expat aid workers and those around them more generally, both geographically and socially. Fears about security, especially material security, also shape how expat aid workers interact with those physically closest to them, their domestic staff. Their relationship to their staff is thus a delicate dance of getting close enough to win loyalty and develop trust but creating boundaries so as not to be vulnerable to theft or a patronage relationship that makes them uncomfortable. The consequences of the distancing work of security are a less integrative and immersive experience for foreign aid workers and a more vulnerable and precarious position for domestic workers.

SECURITIZATION AND AID

Researchers have described a significant shift in the way that the aid industry perceives the safety and security of its employees in the field. In the past twenty to twenty-five years, there has been a consistent increase in the amount of aid agency resources invested in ensuring that their staff are physically safe (Smirl 2015, 58). Researchers are dubious about the extent to which this shift is related to a genuinely heightened risk rather than merely a *perceived* increase in risk.[1] Stoddard, Harmer, and DiDomenico (2008) looked at the Aid Worker Security Database, a global tracker of attacks against aid workers and discovered that although there has been a trend of increased attacks, this increase was concentrated in extremely high-risk environments. From 2006 to 2008, for example, almost three quarters of all recorded attacks took place in only six countries: Afghanistan, Somalia, Chad, Pakistan, Sudan, and Sri Lanka (207). Furthermore, most were not random criminal attacks but were perpetrated by known opposition groups with known political motives (208).

Despite this specific context, a "bunkerization" (Duffield 2010) has taken place in all contexts of aid work. As a result, aid workers lead more and more securitized lives. Though some contexts are more bunkerized than others, with aid workers in conflict areas leading the entirety of their work and residential lives behind fortress walls with barbed wire, heightened security measures have grown up across all aid locations. This is true even for workers in relatively safe areas like Dakar, where security measures include guards for their homes and offices,[2] living in designated safe neighborhoods and in securitized dwellings, and modifying their behavior through field security trainings[3] and other norms and practices that nurture a culture of fear.

Drążkiewicz-Grodzicka (2018) argues that security issues and perceptions of the field as a place of risk are institutionalized. She contends that NGOs themselves, through safety procedures, policies, and plans, produce a "truth" about the danger of the mission site. Aid workers are told and begin to embody the idea that underdevelopment and poverty are inherently dangerous and scary and specifically threatening to aid workers.

This mentality has multiple consequences for aid workers' understandings of their work. Roth (2015) has noted that many workers themselves view aid work as "edgework," something that gives them adrenalin because of its inherent risk.[4] Drążkiewicz-Grodzicka (2018) believes the culture of securitization, in addition to specific behaviors and attitudes around risk and safety, are not a reaction to actual conditions so much as a means for employers to govern the lives of aid workers, allowing organizations to structure and manipulate the outside-of-work hours for their employees in the name of protecting their safety.

For both Smirl (2015) and Duffield (2010), who examine how this securitization is shaped by space and place, a key result of bunkerization is that aid workers are further removed from the people they serve. Their lifestyles become more bounded and isolated as they stick to areas and behaviors deemed safe. Not only are they behind high walls and barbed wire, but they also feel the need to distance themselves and retreat from what they perceive as a dangerous environment. As Duffield puts it, "The perception of heightened danger means that an increasingly segregated aid environment has been embraced more than it has been imposed" (478).

Of course, this is another issue where disparities between expatriate aid workers and local hires is stark. Few of these security measures extend to local hires. Most of the measures, like fortressed exterior walls of their homes and agency-funded security guards patrolling them, are deemed unnecessary for local staff. Some protocols and recommendations (such as "don't eat local street food") are clearly absurdly inappropriate for local hires. These discrepancies only add to the obstacles for expat cultural integration and solidarity or closeness with their local colleagues.

The securitization measures of the big international aid agencies promote a "social, intellectual and emotional withdrawal" (Duffield 2010, 478) from the societies in which they work as essential for safety in a context of permanent threat. This is the case even in places like Dakar, where aid workers generally don't feel the threat to be immediate. Amanda, an aid worker in the field of nutrition and food security described her experience posted in a compound in Afghanistan as particularly difficult because she was able to interact with only the Afghanis who worked in her office and was never allowed to walk the streets freely or visit them in their homes. "If you go in wanting close connection with the community and wanting all the things that people in aid want—wanting to know the country and feel connected," then such a cloistered experience could be depressing. "We all are in this business because we want that to a certain extent," she asserted.

To what extent aid workers seek out a close to connection to their community of work is a question aid workers often discuss. Amanda had, for example, never visited her Dakar colleagues in their homes in her two years in Senegal, despite no prohibition on doing so. Concern about living in an expat "bubble" or "island" (Verma 2011, 72) instead of integrating into daily life of local people echoed throughout my interviews and interactions with expat aid workers, yet aid workers make efforts to create and stay within a bubble at the same time that they lament it.

The designation of certain parts of a city as "safe for expats" draws them and businesses targeted toward them and effectively shapes the city. This is certainly the case with Les Almadies, the beachside neighborhood where so many of my expat aid interlocutors lived, worked, ate, and drank. Walking through the Almadies, where expats are so visible, a white person can feel almost in the majority; walking-while-white does not feel nearly as conspicuous as in other parts of the city. As in other contexts of aid work, "instead of living and interacting with the communities they have come to assist, aid workers are drawn towards other internationals or 'expats' and rarely move beyond a small number of hotels, restaurants, offices and compounds" (Smirl 2015, xii). In Dakar, expat aid workers have shaped the social, commercial, and real estate landscape of the neighborhoods that cater to them—like Les Almadies, Fann, Mermoz, Pointe E, Hann, and Mamelles.

Since it became an urban center, Dakar has always had neighborhoods that were coded white; in fact, the neighborhoods listed above have been inhabited by Western residents for over a century. Through never officially following an explicit policy of racial segregation, French colonial administration also used the rational of safety, in that case sanitation and contagion, to effectively cordon off some areas of the city for Europeans and others for Africans.[5] The pretext of a hygiene obsession was used to unofficially enforce a racial segregation that might otherwise have been hard to square with republican French values that officially decried racism and counted Dakar as one of the four communes of Senegal, in which *originaires* were granted French citizenship rights.[6]

So stark was the character of white neighborhoods in the colonial period that one anthropologist visiting colonial Dakar remarked of one of the exemplary neighborhoods of white Dakar, the Plateau, that there were few African faces in the neighborhood's cafés, bars, restaurants, and hotels. He mused that "the visitor who only spends a few hours in Dakar might reasonably wonder whether he was in Africa at all" (Gorer 1935, 74).

In contemporary Senegal, concerns for safety, security, and sanitation again maintain the de facto "dual city" of racial segregation (Bigon 2016, 119). Because European areas of Dakar were prioritized for health and safety infrastructure as well as Western-style living, with spacious walled family homes, these neighborhoods remain the most desirable and thus most costly places to live. Though elite Senegalese share these upper-class neighborhoods with expats now, their character remains still defined by their association with Western residence (366) and buffered from the more crowded and chaotic parts of the city that even then were set aside by colonial urban planners for Africans. These are primarily the neighborhoods where domestic workers for expats live.

The neighborhoods where domestic workers for expats live, like Dakar's large banlieue and the crowded *quartiers populaires* of Fass and the Medina, by contrast, do not offer the same large villas and quiet residential boulevards of the neighborhoods where aid workers live, but were built for density. They often suffer from flooding due to a lack of effective sewer systems and their access to garbage collection is much less reliable. During Dakar's garbage strikes and crises, the poorer neighborhoods are more likely to suffer from pileups of stinking, rotting waste, whereas the elite areas negotiate their own private waste collection or use their influence to make special arrangements from the state (Fredericks 2018, 10).

Frantz Fanon (1963, 39) painted a vivid picture of the inequities of colonial cities in his description of the "native town" versus the "colonial world" of the white settler. The native town

> is a world without spaciousness; men live there on top of each other, and their huts are built one on top of the other. The native town is a hungry town, starved of bread, of meat, of shoes, of coal, of light. The native town is a crouching village, a town on its knees, a town wallowing in the mire.

The white settler's town is, on the other hand,

a brightly lit town; the streets are covered with asphalt, and the garbage cans swallow all the leavings, unseen, unknown and hardly thought about. The settler's feet are never visible, except perhaps in the sea; but there you're never close enough to see them. His feet are protected by strong shoes although the streets of his town are clean and even, with no holes or stones. The settler's town is a well-fed town, an easygoing town; its belly is always full of good things. The settlers' town is a town of white people, of foreigners.

As more and more residential buildings in upper-class neighborhoods that market to Western expats and their security needs are constructed—some explicitly built in line with the expectations of foreign embassies and international NGOs, including high walls and generators—the city retains a kind of segregation by class and race. Elite enclaves are insulated from some of the most glaring examples of poverty and infrastructural failure, and thus those living within them are buffered from not only experiencing these challenges but fully witnessing, understanding, and acknowledging them.

A PLACE WHERE ONE CAN WALK AT NIGHT

Though they selected an apartment in an expat enclave based on its security, Brian and Erin, like many expat aid workers in Senegal, had lived in contexts more dangerous than Dakar. Indeed, many of my aid worker interlocutors spoke of feeling much safer in Dakar than in previous postings in Nairobi or Johannesburg, for example. Some had lived in contexts with curfews and strict security orders or even inside compounds in places of high security risk like Juba, South Sudan, or Kabul, Afghanistan. Nevertheless, aid workers in Dakar thought and talked about personal security as a matter of course, in ways that reflect the trend in international aid agencies to give security greater attention.

Dakar is a relatively sleepy town as far as security threats go. Most expats move freely throughout the city, including after dark.

Though most expat homes and the homes of the wealthy local elite are guarded by private security guards, these guards are generally not armed beyond a nightstick, and although many expat homes are behind security walls, few have security cameras, alarm systems, or other safety measures that expats use as a matter of course in places like Cape Town, South Africa. In Dakar, aid workers do not actively worry about carjackings and other forms of violent crime. Few expats I interviewed or those they knew had experienced violent crime in Dakar, and such incidents were mostly low-level street crimes—a few muggings and purse snatchings and one home invasion that was non-violent, although the perpetrator was carrying a machete.

More systematic or state-sponsored violence is also not a worry in Dakar. Senegal has enjoyed relative politically stability since independence in 1960,[7] with peaceful transfers of power after mostly democratic elections. The country is 95 percent Muslim, though its government is secular and the population is religiously moderate. In the wake of extremist terrorism in Mali, Burkina Faso, and Ivory Coast in 2016, Senegal has worked closely with the US military and other Western nations to build its counterterrorism program, forming the specialized Inter-Ministerial Framework for Intervention and Coordination of Counterterrorism Operations (CICO) and training its military police and national police to detect, deter, and prevent terrorist activity.[8]

Expats in Dakar were aware of heightened security, particularly after the Ouagadougou, Burkina Faso, attack, which sent shock waves through the region. In mid-January 2016, a terrorist group with links to al-Qaeda laid siege to a luxury hotel—a popular hangout for Western expats—in Burkina Faso's capital, killing at least thirty people and wounding over one hundred more (Kibora 2019). European, Canadian, and American citizens were among the dead. A similar attack took place in March in a beach town outside Abidjan, the capital of Ivory Coast (Madore 2016). In the wake of these attacks, the Senegalese government issued an ultimatum to Senegalese hotels to improve their security or face closure. The federal government itself provided additional armed police for certain hotels, including the upscale Radisson Blu Hotel on the city's beachside Corniche.

Aid workers who were in Dakar at the time remember haphazard attempts to heighten security across the city. Rumors of a planned terrorist attack by sea on a coastal hotel and casino meant that USAID and other US embassy employees were forbidden to dine at beachside restaurants for about a month.[9] This policy's influence did not last long, however, and people returned to the beachside restaurants that are so popular with expats. One USAID employee recalled that after an initial period of compliance, most Americans in Dakar felt comfortable disobeying these orders as a sense of normalcy returned. "After a while they were just like, 'This is dumb,'" she remembered. "Or it's just impractical."

Most expat aid workers do not worry about terrorism on a daily basis, feel safe driving and walking around Senegal, and do not feel like targets of physical violence.[10] Jessica, whose whole family had been robbed at gunpoint in their home in Nairobi, said she had to adjust to the safer conditions in Dakar. "It's so much more relaxed here," she told me as we ate grapefruit and avocado salads by the ocean at a beachside restaurant. "Like in every way. Which I think is great in some respects, but in other respects might not be great." At first, she said that she had trouble letting her guard down. "It definitely took me a while. I realized after a while that I just had to adapt. And then I was like, 'Wow, I didn't realize how much it was really affecting me until here, where I felt less of it.'" "Now," she said, laughing, "I've probably relaxed too much."

Gwyneth said working in Juba, the capital of South Sudan, where conditions were very securitized due to ongoing conflict, also messed with what she called her "safety radar." "I had to recalibrate slightly," she said, of moving to Dakar. She recalled being home for a visit to her native UK and "walking around at 9 o'clock in the dark and going, 'Oh my god, I should be home by now,' because I got so used to having a curfew and it just not being okay to walk anywhere at times. And I'm like, 'You're in Hartfordshire, Gwyneth. It's quite all right to be walking around in the dark. It's like 9:00, 9:30. You know, there are people walking around with their children! It's okay.'"

This posture of extreme vigilance is part of the new reality of aid work. Gwyneth and others have been trained to think of their surroundings as full of threat not only through organizational procedure but also through "very specific behaviors and attitudes which are actively, though informally, promoted" (Drążkiewicz-Grodzicka 2018, 816).[11] But like Jessica, Gwyneth feels safer in Dakar than in previous posts. She feels safe walking at night in most parts of Dakar and comfortable taking taxis at night.

Feeling comfortable walking, whether at day or night, was an important indicator of safety for many of my interlocutors, especially women. "Sometimes I walk even at night," Kim, a French-American aid worker exclaimed as evidence of Dakar's relative safety. "In Tanzania you couldn't walk, even during the day." Of course, in Tanzania most people do walk during the day. But many expats avoid it because of worries for their safety. As an expat, they feel exposed to threat much more than locals because they are highly visible as a presumably monied target. This "fishbowl syndrome" (Verma 2011, 69) is a common complaint especially for white aid workers in Africa, and their visibility does not decrease with length of stay. Still, those in Senegal operate with a kind of precaution that far exceeds the realities of security in Dakar. Kim, despite her sense of safety walking at night in Dakar, lives in an apartment building where all the other tenants are expats, guarded by a group of uniformed security guards, and works in a fortresslike, walled-off compound also guarded by uniformed security guards.

FORTRESSLIKE CARS

An ability to walk, though prized, does not mean expats travel primarily on foot. Generally, expat aid workers travel by car. An SUV is the car of choice for many aid workers in Dakar, not only for their personal car but also for work, such as the ubiquitous white aid SUVs with an NGO logo on the side. SUVs, emblematic of international aid work across the developing world, are one of the "bounded and increasingly securitized spaces of international aid workers" (Smirl 2015, 5).

Some of the aid workers I interviewed had had personal chauffeurs in other countries where they'd been posted, but few found them necessary in Dakar. Those few who had them usually used them to ferry their kids to and from school and other activities while they and their spouse were at work. Gemma had employed a driver in Uganda but drove herself in Senegal. She had been in a car accident in her first month in Dakar. She had been sideswiped by, as she put it, "one of those colorful vans—I forget what you call them." She was referring to the *kaar rapide*, a painted van that is the symbol of Senegal (figure 1). That after four years, she would need me to supply the name of this omnipresent vehicle of public transport in Senegal is indicative of how SUVs, like walled compounds, can create a certain distance and remove from daily urban life.

As Smirl (2015) explains, the SUV "changes the experience that the aid worker has of the physical environment and climate. Instead

FIGURE 1. The *kaar rapide*, a type of public transportation in Dakar that is widely used in iconography of the country. Photo by Ricci Shryock.

of being exposed to heat, rain, dust, the aid worker can ride along in a climate-controlled environment" (104), happily remaining in the more comfortable of Fanon's two cities. The SUV is more than just a buffer, according to Smirl: "It may allow the passengers to move at a higher velocity than the majority of other people around them, introducing a level of inequality of movement, and possibly making movement for those on foot, bike, motorcycle, horse or even lower, older cars more dangerous" (104).

Gemma recounted that she didn't even get out of her car after the *kaar rapide* crashed into and crushed her front bumper. She was driving her daughter back from a horseback-riding lesson in the early evening right after sundown. "I had both kids in the car and I was like, 'In the end, do I really believe this guy has insurance or is going to pay me?'" She laughed. "My husband was like, 'Did you stop?' And I was like, 'What would that have gotten me?' I had no confidence that that was going to get me anywhere, and I didn't want to leave the kids in the car—it was night time. I didn't want to get out of the car with the kids there and all that. So I just left."

Like other US federal employees who work overseas, Gemma had to take a State Department defensive driving course as part of her Foreign Service counter-terrorism training. This course trains employees for a quick getaway, how to take control of a car if the driver is incapacitated, and how to ram another car out of the way if it is blocking the path. A similar course given to UN employees includes training about what to do in case of a carjacking or a hostage situation (Duffield 2010). These trainings take for granted that employees may be put in life-threatening scenarios while on overseas posts and ensure their employees will be prepared to confront danger wherever they go.

Gemma had another road accident a few years later, when a taxi rear-ended her after she stopped to let a pedestrian cross. "He crashed into the back of me, which didn't hurt my car at all—I have a Honda Pilot—but it crunched his, broke his front left headlight." She got out and saw that there was no damage to her SUV so she was tempted to leave. "He got out of his car and his was broken but—so I was like, 'This is a little awkward because I don't know . . . and usually taxi drivers don't speak French.' I couldn't communicate with him anyway." A crowd started to form around the scene of the accident. "So all these people came, and they're all speaking—in Wolof, presumably—and I didn't understand what was going on, but I didn't want to just leave the scene because I didn't want everyone to get pissed at me."

Eventually (though after nearly four years, her familiarity with the local lingua franca, Wolof, was not good enough for her to confidently recognize it), Gemma was able to determine that the crowd was yelling at the taxi driver and not her because they recognized that he was in the wrong. What followed next was also revealing of expat life in Dakar. "Thankfully, there was actually a car that came by with foreigners in it, and they stopped and they were like, 'Are you okay?' Some white people came by and they were like, 'Are you okay?' And I didn't know who they were, where they were from. And I was like, 'Yeah, I'm fine.'" Gemma could only imagine what they were thinking as they drove by and saw her "there, alone, in the middle of this, like, traffic mess." By "alone," she meant as the only white person in a crowd shouting what she presumed was Wolof.

The crowd apparently saw things this way as well. "I was waiting for someone to kind of tell me what was going on, and so finally one guy was just like, 'Ma'am, you should just go. He would not be doing this if you were not white. He's in the wrong.' And I was like, 'Okay, fine.'" Gemma's visibility with her white skin meant not only that she was a potential target of this driver's misplaced blame but also that she was seen by white strangers and by Senegalese onlookers alike as vulnerable, worthy of respect, protection, and assistance and absolved from having to wait around to discuss the details or talk to police.

Lisa Smirl (2015) has said of the SUV that it represents physical safety to humanitarian workers not only because of its visibility and solid build but also as a representation of "the protection that has historically been derived from its symbolic values of neutrality, impartiality and universality." She notes, however, that this is not how it is perceived by local communities. "To the Third World, it has arguably come to represent the petroleum-fueled inequality that has led to a situation in which a self-appointed few behave in a way which damages their surroundings and others" (101).[12]

A country office director of a large faith-based NGO said her organization—in contrast to other aid organizations—had thought meaningfully about the way that the image of aid work and the perception of the white SUV impacts the reception of aid workers and their mission. "We pass the message to our staff that even, for example, the drivers have to stop to let people pass. Because you're representing [the NGO]." She noted that this issue of reputation is itself a security issue: "You want to be safe in places; you want people to trust you, and you want people to know that if [this NGO] is there, it's going to be a good thing. And we will establish a good relationship. And in many places where we have issues, it is the local communities that have protected us. So, it's a security issue."

OFFICE AS FORTRESS

Lori suggested that I meet her at her office for our interview. Lori works for USAID, so her office is inside the US embassy. The USAID office in Dakar used to be separate from the embassy, which had been situated on Avenue Jean XXIII, a lively street in the center of downtown Dakar, since the 1960s. In 2013, as part of a group of sweeping US State Department and Department of Defense changes worldwide, the embassy was moved to the posh Point des Almadies, near one the fanciest hotels in town, then called Le Méridien Président, now the King Fahd Palace Hotel. The US embassy, in a perfect bit of symbolism, took over land that had belonged to the old Club Med on the westernmost tip of West Africa. On that site, they built a state-of-the-art, LEED-certified compound, and the USAID offices moved inside it.[13]

Lori told me I would need to bring my US passport to get into the embassy to meet with her, so I was prepared as I walked up to the security booth full of more than half a dozen private security guards in uniform, as well as a few US Marines. I stated my purpose and handed over my passport. After ten full minutes of perusing my passport and making phone calls, they buzzed me inside to the antechamber. I emptied the contents of my bag into a bin for the airport-style conveyer belt screening and walked through the metal detector. The security guards wanted to confiscate my phone and recording device. I pushed back, saying that I needed to record my interview. We went back and forth about this, and finally they called Lori to come out and escort me, as visitors must be accompanied everywhere, even the restroom. I told her of my recording device dilemma, and she negotiated with the guard in elementary French and with a good deal of exasperation. I was handed back my recording device, though the rest of my electronics were confiscated, as is the security rule, and Lori escorted me into the building with an apology. "They are so strict about the dumbest things," she said.

In the lobby of the fancy new embassy building, I saw an old friend, a Senegalese employee of the US embassy whom I had known for years, since she ran study-abroad programs for American undergraduates. She greeted me warmly with her fluent English and we chatted for a bit about our lives and our kids. She told me of a recent trip to Washington, DC, where she'd seen a mutual friend. Lori then suggested we do our interview outside in the embassy's quiet Zen garden within the security walls. We sat among the vibrant green grass and shady trees—a rare thing to see in the Sahel—and talked about Lori's experiences in Dakar.

Lori and her husband, both USAID employees, lived close to the embassy, but they usually took taxis to work because they would be too dusty and sweaty for a professional environment were they to walk the two kilometers from home to the office. "I would need too many outfits!" Lori offered by way of explanation, laughing. After work, Lori worked out at the embassy gym (which has its own swimming pool) and left the walled compound to head home to make dinner with her husband in their apartment on the fourth floor of an apartment building full of US embassy employees, guarded by uniformed guards from the same agency that guards her fortresslike work building.

For grocery shopping, Lori would have her maid buy fish, because she was intimidated by the process locally, and she had milk, yogurt, and chicken delivered to her home for her maid to receive while she and her husband were at work. She bought her other fresh groceries in the parking lot of the embassy building. Twice a week, vegetable and fruit merchants who were given special clearance and dispensation by the embassy came into the embassy compound and sold their wares at moderately inflated prices to the employees of the US government. Around the winter holidays, handicraft salespeople came to sell gifts like scarfs and baskets within the compound.

All this meant Lori had limited interactions with Senegal as a country. Her Senegalese colleagues, like my friend who I ran into at the embassy, generally spoke English and had been working in a US work environment for years. Even if she had wanted to eavesdrop on their conversations with each other, she couldn't, as she was trained in French by the State Department, not in her colleagues' language of choice for casual banter, Wolof. Lori had limited and perfunctory interactions with taxi drivers and security guards. Her maid had worked in American households for over a decade and was familiar with the intricacies of an American household, from making Western-style dinners to using the large, US-imported washers and dryers common to all USAID residences.

As a former Peace Corps volunteer who served in South America, Lori was aware that she was not doing the kind of hands-on work she used to do. "I just feel like ever since I left the Peace Corps, I've been getting further and further from the work. And it kills me a little bit. But then, I know why I'm here. I know what my job is—you know what I mean?" Her job was to deal with the macro-level finance portfolio, not to work alongside community partners. Though she found it professionally fulfilling and recognized the kind of impact this role gave her, she acknowledged the disconnect between herself and the people around her. "We are bureaucrats. I'm a technical bureaucrat, that's absolutely true. And I think we try to do our part, but we are in that building that you have to get through eight doors to get through."

Thomas Dichter, a career USAID employee, toured fourteen USAID offices on three continents in 2016 and came to similar findings to those of scholars like Smirl and Duffield. In an article for the *Foreign Service Journal*, which was much discussed among USAID employees in Dakar while I was there interviewing, Dichter (2016) reported that "USAID's American personnel formed very few meaningful local relationships and tended to be uninformed or misinformed about local organizations and trends." He discussed the real implications this disconnect has for the work and how it directly sabotages USAID's stated goal of working more closely and more directly with local organizations and local governments. If the USAID personnel don't feel connected or in tune with local partners, they are much less likely to turn over the reins and accounts to them. Local partners, for their part, grow frustrated with an ever-changing cast of Americans who need to be reeducated from scratch when they transition in every three or four years.

For USAID employees, expected to conform to security rules and heavy workloads, it was difficult to find a way around this isolation. This was true for UN employees as well, who had similar amenities, infrastructures, and workloads abroad. Employees of smaller NGOs felt that they lived closer to the ground but still lamented their "toubab bubble." Routinely, aid workers said they had real contact with only a handful of Senegalese people: their domestic workers. These relationships are not exempt from the securitization concerns, however. Indeed, they are in many ways shaped by them.

PROPERTY CRIME AND SECURITY STAFF

Though aid workers in Senegal did not generally worry about being targets of violence or terrorism, they did worry regularly about property crime, including the pettiest of thefts. Smirl (2015) notes that being a wealthy expat and thus a "highly visible" person can play tricks with the mind, even if that visibility is not necessarily negative. "You begin to think that everything is about you, and may interpret things in a skewed way" (99). If you worry, like Erin and Brian did, that even a glimpse into your living conditions could invite theft and danger, everyday interactions become fraught. This low-level anxiety has direct implications for relations with house staff, as the remainder of the chapter will address.

Most expats have some form of security guard for their residence, as well as for their office. Some hire their own personal guard; sometimes their employer has a service that they contract with that assigns uniformed guards to their home. Others inherit a security guard that comes with the residence, whether an apartment complex or a single-family dwelling. Some have night guards only, but many have guards both day and night.

A guard's official responsibility is to sit outside the home or office (figure 2), stay awake, and be vigilant against any criminality. The use value of guards is generally more as a deterrent through their presence than any actual policing of the neighborhood. Guards' commitment to their job obviously varies greatly. As I noted in the previous chapter, it is not unusual for guards to perform other duties than simply guarding the building, such as running errands, washing cars, walking dogs, cleaning, and gardening. In the small NGO I worked for, the night guard also served as the receptionist when the rest of the staff had gone home for the day, answering phones and giving out information. Some privately hired guards live in the buildings they guard, usually in small spaces like sheds or garages.

The UN, the US embassy, and other organizations contract with private security firms in Dakar, like SAGAM International. SAGAM

FIGURE 2. Security guard at his post outside a villa in Dakar. Photo by Ricci Shryock.

was founded in 1985 and in addition to other security services like transporting cash and valuables, it is known for its provision of uniformed guards. These guards dress in identical blue military-like uniforms (figure 3), get regular inspections, and have very specific rules to follow about their conduct and protocols for keeping the property secure. They are regularly rotated to different houses or buildings after a matter of months so as to avoid complacency and the forming of close attachments. At the time of my writing, SAGAM guards made about 90,000 CFA francs ($150) per month, in addition to what is called the thirteenth month—a bonus of one month's pay at the end of every year—as well as some minor health insurance benefits and access to small emergency loans. Independently hired guards make considerably less money, starting at 35,000 CFA francs per month (roughly $60), and often for longer work hours with even more flexible job descriptions.

FIGURE 3. SAGAM security guard on the job. Photo by Ricci Shryock.

The International Federation of the Red Cross and Red Crescent Societies produces guidelines for the employment of security guards when its employees are stationed abroad. These include not only respecting local labor laws but also briefing the guards on the mission of the organization and the values it holds. "Describe to the guards the kind of reputation we wish to develop among the local population," the guidelines advise. "Make sure the guards understand that their role is not only to protect the office, warehouse or residence, but also to protect the image of the International Federation. Encourage them to feel part of the delegation" (IFRC 2011).

When I talked with guards who watched over aid workers' residences, however, I found they had little awareness of their employers' employment. Many did not know whether their employers were in business, development, or diplomacy. Neither the guards nor their employers seemed compelled to converse about this kind of information, even when they had familiar or friendly relations.

Erin and Brian's guards were employed by the landlord of their building, included as part of their rent. Besides not letting them in the apartment, the couple had other rules for boundary making with their guards, reflecting the awkward intimacy of the relationship with people who are always present in the exterior space of your home but are not family, friends, or co-workers. When I said that I had given the guard a little tip for bringing my bag up the stairs, they were again concerned and wanted to know how much. They were glad it was only the equivalent of a couple of dollars, so as not to set the wrong precedent. They went on to tell me that that particular guard routinely asks for money to buy himself tea, which is a source of annoyance to them. They occasionally brought the guards food when they made extra for dinner, but they were bothered by direct appeals for cash.

In interviews, many aid workers emphasized their camaraderie with their guards, with anecdotes about bringing them gifts from trips overseas, sharing food with them on holidays, and inviting them and their children to birthday parties at their home. They also told stories, however, about the dangers and discomforts of getting too close to guards.

Carly, who worked in communications for a local NGO in Dakar, felt extreme frustration when her guard would ask her and her husband for money. "He asked for money all the time. Like constantly. And it got to the point where you felt like, 'Okay, he's not even interested in being friends with us or interested our family, he's just in this because we're white people that can give him money.'" Here, Carly indicated her expectation that her guard might take the job guarding her home for under $150 a month out of friendship or a concern for her family. She implied that friendship with a guard was an appropriate kind of intimate interaction, but the request for money—highlighting the social distance between her family and her guard—was hurtful to her. Certain kinds of intimacy, like friendship, would be welcome, but the explicit kind of patron-client relationship that the guard tried to establish was a problem. Such requests highlighted the reality of the wealth disparity that made her able to employ this guard and made him accept such tedious and underpaid work—and that reality made Carly uncomfortable.

Boundary making and rule setting were common strategies by expat employers of domestic workers who seemed anxious to disavow the huge chasm between the resources they possessed and the resources possessed by everyone around them. The anxiety of falling into a pattern of giving when asked was a popular refrain from employers who rightly understood that there would be no point when they didn't "have" the money and the domestic worker—or, in fact, many Senegalese people around them—didn't "need" it. Expats adopted strange and arbitrary practices in relation to this discomfiting reality. One of these was trying to hide their wealth by, for example, not allowing guards in the building or by hiding or downplaying other kinds of lavish consumption. Another was making arbitrary rules about what they would give money for and what they wouldn't, what requests they would grant and what ones they would refuse, that allowed them to avoid feeling taken advantage of. This mirrored in some ways the behavior of aid agencies themselves toward the populations with whom they work: we will fund girls' education because we believe it leads to development, but we refuse to give money to the Ministry of Education because of corruption. We will magisterially decide what your "real" needs are and how our money should be used for them.

Meredith, a gender-based-violence expert working for the UN, recalled her discomfort in multiple incidents of being asked by chauffeurs for sums of money, because of her personal gendered philosophy of charitable giving: "I don't—it sounds bad—but I don't like giving money to men, you know, like it's a cliché, but I don't feel good about what they are going to use it on." She remembered an incident where she did say yes to a direct request from a chauffeur, mostly, she said, because she was returning from a visit to the field and recalled being very tired and grateful to the driver for taking her straight to her home. "He said he needed 5,000 to give his daughter *medicaments* or something like that and I just gave it to him, and I remember the next morning being kind of pissed. I felt guiltiness that I was pissed, but I'm also like, 'I know you don't make a lot of money, but you do have a job.'" Though Meredith acknowledges that the driver's salary was quite low, she felt his inability to have prioritized his daughter's health in his own savings reflected poor judgment, perhaps of the kind she alluded to as typical of men.

An employee of a major religious NGO explained that she and her husband did not simply give extra money when their security guards requested it. They insisted on giving loans that were to be repaid, "to try and reinforce the understanding that you're not just getting money for free," she explained, as well as to help them to become better managers of their finances. This lesson in money management, she believed, would do more good for her employees' future than any handout.

An American employee of USAID said she had to fire her gardener because she felt he wasn't being transparent. "I want the relationship with them to be like, 'I can give them money to go buy something and feel like they're going to buy the thing at a good price and also give me change and maybe let me know the price. And I'll let them keep the change.' But I want them to be transparent about what's going on. And he wasn't." This woman didn't care about the dollar or two that was not being returned to her, but rather wanted to feel that she was in control of the choice of whether or not to be benevolent with that money, which she was convinced she would be.

Tamara had not found a happy personal rapport with her guards and this bothered her. "They're not very talkative, these guards. I try to say good morning and build relationships with them, you know? He had a son and I found out about it like five days later, and I'm like 'You didn't tell me!' You know? But we try to keep some sort of, like, bond relationships," she says, indicating a desire echoed across aid workers to have some semblance of a bounded intimacy with guards.

A "bounded intimacy," coined by Elizabeth Bernstein (2007) in a very different context, is a kind of intimacy that is contingent and has boundaries that one party controls.

Carly said that she and her husband were partly to blame for tensions with their guard, as they had made the mistake of giving the guard money for the first few times he requested some. "You want a good relationship with these people," she explained, "but . . ." A good relationship is imperative with the people you interact with every day and on whom you rely as your first line of defense against would-be intruders. Finding this "good relationship," which balances friendliness and professional distance in a context of severe financial inequalities, is tricky and there is no clear, standardized rule book for this relationship. "Do we get the guards gifts?" one expat asked me—a relative stranger—in an interview that took place in mid-December. "And for which holiday?" she wanted to know. For Christmas because we celebrate it, or for Tamxarit, a Muslim holiday, also known as the day of Ashura, because they celebrate it? Is a gift better than cash? she asked. Others told me about their gift-giving practices or hours or salaries and looked to me to confirm whether theirs were normal or in line with what others were doing.

Indeed, many interviewees expressed a great deal of unease and confusion about the "rules" and best practices for relationships with their guards. Others told me, proudly or as a matter of course, details that intimated some kind of rapport. One UN employee said that he'd been paying for medical expenses of a former guard who was too sick to continue with his work. "I don't know if he had a heart issue. He had something that was quite serious." Several pleaded with the security agency not to fire favorite guards who had been caught sleeping at their posts, usually to no avail. Another told me in detail which kinds of track suits she had brought back for her guards after a trip to the US and to how much trouble she'd gone hunting them down on her vacation. Fiona's family was particularly close to their night guard and so when her husband switched from one NGO job to another job that came with assigned guards from an agency, they created a new position for their old guard as a driver, gardener, and childminder so as not to lose him.

Fiona had not been impressed with the new guards from the agency and had not been afraid to express that displeasure to the agency. "Respect and tolerance and good manners are very important to us in the house," she told me over cappuccinos in a patisserie near her home in Almadies. "There've been two occasions where I've been unhappy with the kind of comportment of the guards so I was like, 'This guy's doing this and this,' and the agency removed the guards from their posts. Slouching in the chair, sitting inside. Like, there's a rule: When we're in the house, they're outside. When we're not in the house, they can be outside with the gate locked. But it's very simple." Slouching in her chair to demonstrate her guard's unacceptable behavior, she continued, "And just a big attitude, kind of a too-cool-for-school, one guy, and I was like 'What's your name?'" She mumbles in a gruff voice, "'Abdoulaye.' And I was like, 'Okay, you're sleeping there.' And he was kind of thrown back in his seat. And [the driver] had told him, 'Don't let Madame see you like that.' Yeah, 'smarten yourself up a bit.' So I saw it and went to [my husband] and said, 'No, everybody else is killing themselves around the house. You know, they have a'—Dinah, we don't push them." She interrupted herself to clarify, concerned she had painted too harsh a picture of her exacting demands as an employer. "They come in, they take a long breakfast. It's very social. But everything is done in the house that needs to be done." For Fiona, what she expected from a guard was the same thing she expected from the three other domestic workers in her employ: professionalism and hard work.

It is sometimes hard to assess hard work when the job is simply guarding (see, for instance, figure 2). This may be why guards end up walking dogs, washing cars, and doing other odd jobs around the house. Many aid workers spoke of guards falling asleep on the job or wandering off from their posts. Or simply being too present and in the way. Having guards around all the time in your space can be an uncomfortable way to live.

Rayna admitted the relationship with guards was a bit strange for her. She complained that the agency her organization hired rotated the guards too frequently and so she could not hang onto the ones she liked. "We have some guards now who are just . . . a little annoying. Some guards are great. Some just get on my nerves because I find that they don't . . . they're just sitting there not doing their job." Another guard scared her. "He was tall and gruff, and I felt uncomfortable around him." He left the job after a short time, and when the tires of her family's four bikes were punctured, she suspected him. She didn't know for sure that it was him, and she couldn't think of anything she would have done in his short tenure to have made him do this to her family, but because he never showed up again, he remained her number-one suspect.

Rayna said that some interactions with guards had been positive. "Sometimes when I get a really good feeling about them, we'll bring them food," she recounted, but she had had other moments of discomfort and annoyance with the men who were in her space. "Like, I felt really bad because one time I got really upset at one of them. Because I kept going out and in and he kept locking the door. And I'm like, 'You see I'm going in and out of the house!' But they're like so quick to lock the door. And I'm like, 'Stop locking the door!' Just . . . like, 'You're standing here,' like, 'You don't have to lock it all the time.' So I was kind of like . . ." she trailed off, a bit embarrassed. "I kinda got a little frustrated and I said something in English. I said, 'Why are you being such an idiot?' And my husband was like, 'Rayna, that word is universal, you shouldn't say that.' But I was kind of mumbling it and then I felt bad, so . . . I can't remember if I said sorry to him . . . so I'm like extra nice to him now because I . . . you know, they're taking care of our house." Rayna and her husband know that they depend on the guards to protect their home and thus should maintain pleasant relations with them. Their intimate knowledge in the space of their home makes Rayna feel vulnerable to guards who may threaten their safety or return and destroy their property, even if it is simply bike tires.

Like Fiona, Tamara also had trouble with her guards and had two of them dismissed from their agency. "In the beginning, I'm not really sure what the protocol was, but they would do things like just walk people up to my front door. And my door's a glass door, so, you know. There's a gate but they would let them in and then just walk them all the way up to my house, which has a full glass door, without checking whether I wanted a visitor." Tamara repeatedly emphasizes the glass door, implying her exposure and the visibility and thus vulnerability of herself and her belongings. "And a couple of times it was people I didn't know that were just like being brought into my house and I was just like, 'Um, yeah, you need to leave.' But they would just walk them to my door. I'm like, 'You're bringing them to me already. I don't really get a say in this' . . . One time it was some guy who was pulling out his phone and showing me pictures of his child, speaking to me in Wolof on my doorstep, and I kind of panicked a little bit. I was like, 'I don't understand. I don't know who this guy is. Get him away. What's he doing in my house?' So that was a little bit of an issue." Part of a guard's job in Tamara's view was to insulate her from local people arriving on her doorstep—to keep the needy at bay.

Tamara had other issues regarding a lack of vigilance among her guards. "The other time, the guy was, like, sleeping in the middle of the night, or he was never to be found during the day. He just went into the garage room. And would just disappear in the hot season. I was like, 'Okay, you've gotta go.' 'Oh, it was too hot outside' is what he said. 'It was too hot outside.' 'Okay, well you can clearly not be a guard. That's the job. The job is to sit. Outside. Sorry.'" She told the head of security of her NGO, and the guard was immediately switched out.

Another guard regularly abandoned his post as well, and at first Tamara was not sure whether to interpret this as different rules in Senegal for guards than in her previous West African post, Niger.

"Initially, like the guards would walk away, and I don't know what's cultural here and what's . . . not? Was the guard just, like, slacking? But he would disappear for like twenty minutes to get himself a coffee. I had this happen like three times. And I was like, 'WHAT?' I just wasn't sure that's normal, and if I was supposed to be . . . In Niger, they told us very directly, like, 'You're not supposed to do that.' Just cultural differences—what are we supposed to be expecting? So I didn't know." Eventually, Tamara eliminated the guards' need to leave the post. "So I bought them like a hot water heater thing. And I bought them insta-packets of coffee and I was like, 'Now you get to have your coffee here.' But in Niger it would never cross my mind because we're told not to do that. They would never . . ."

Other aid workers noted, too, that new posts meant new negotiations of rules and boundaries with their guards. One pointed out that in her previous post in Thailand, she had been treated with much more respectful distance by her guards. She described hiring workers in Thailand as more of a business transaction. "You didn't get involved with them," she remembered. "And here I think it's a little bit more personal. It's kind of a bigger deal." Figuring out where the boundaries should lie with guards—how friendly is too friendly?—was a source of much preoccupation for many aid workers I spoke to, and the stakes of these relationships varied in importance from simply experiencing discomfort to feeling unsafe, but all in the space of their own home.

THEFT AND TRUSTWORTHINESS

No one that I spoke to had been a victim of theft of property from their home where guards were suspected while they were in Dakar, though one NGO had had its offices robbed and suspected the guards of participation in the crime. Some aid workers had experienced such incidents in other posts, however, and described feelings of deep betrayal as a result. Fiona had experienced a theft in Dakar, not of her own property but that of her other domestic employees. Referring to her adult maid and nanny as "the girls," Fiona recounted, "You know, there was one guard who stole something out of one of the girls' purses. And you could feel they weren't . . . All of a sudden, the doors were locked. I was like, 'What's going on?' And they were like, 'Yeah, this has gone missing.' Because they keep their bags in the garage. So all of a sudden I saw the bags coming into the house, I was like, 'What's going on, guys?' And he was removed."

Many aid workers used their maids and nannies as intermediaries with their guards—asking their maids to get information from guards, sending them to deliver boundary-enforcing new rules and admonitions. Often, maids and nannies functioned *as* guards within the home. Many aid workers noted that their domestic workers took pains to ensure that their employers' property was not taken. Rayna approvingly noted that her maid and nanny policed visitors to the house, such as repairmen. "The women are very protective. If anyone comes in the house, they're following them around." Another said of her maid, "She watches everybody like a hawk! And that's really nice because I can focus on my work and my life." A third raved, "She's actually, like, stricter about that than we are. Like when a technician comes to fix something, she, like, watches. Whereas I am a lot more, like, loopy and distracted."

Carly gave examples of her maid's displays of trustworthiness, "I'm notorious for leaving like 1,000 francs (less than $2) in the pocket of my jeans or whatever. And she's so honest. She's like, she always brings the money out. She's like, 'Oh, I found this in your pants when I was doing the laundry' . . . So I have no qualms at all about trusting her." Rayna had a similar story, "And anytime money is in our pockets and it comes out in the wash, they will put it there and leave it there and show us. And they'll take a picture of something to prove it was there and that's how they found it. They just want to make sure that you never suspect anything. It's cute."

Though Rayna frames this behavior as "cute," these incidents suggest that maids and nannies know that they are often the prime suspects when things go missing. Mariama, who worked as a maid for many different expat families, gets tears in her eyes whenever she talks about the time she was accused of stealing by her American employers. She had not stolen, but her employers were convinced she had and fired her. She was devastated. Because of the word-of-mouth system that keeps maids and nannies employed, rumors of stealing or a bad reference from a previous employer could mean never working again in expat circles.[14] In later jobs, Mariama, too, made sure to take pictures of money she found and gave receipts for everything she bought while shopping for her employers, scrupulously piling up the coins of the change. Employers' satisfaction with this practice[15] reveals the underlying truth of their inherent mistrust of the domestic employees and the perpetual vulnerability of domestic workers to that mistrust.

The unavoidable and undeniable resource inequality between expatriates working in Dakar and almost everyone around them makes for fraught interpersonal relations. Barriers between expats and local people, whether enacted through behavior or constructed in the form of literal walls and uniformed guards or the continued racial segregation of residential neighborhoods established in the colonial era, prevent a more meaningful integration of the people who are in theory sent there to address the concerns of local people.

The etymological definition of *security* is the removal (*se*) of care (*cura*). In fact, however, much of the process of securitization makes people feel less safe. As Yuval-Davis, Wemyss, and Cassidy (2018) point out, "Technologies of everyday bordering, which are supposedly aimed at making people feel safe by keeping those who do not belong out, can undermine feelings of safety for everyone through raising a sense of precarity" (230). This means that aid workers come to view their position as one of insecurity and, as others have found, "The fear of crime can result in mistrust towards others and limit the ability to form social ties" (Faeth and Kittler 2017, 399). The borders between aid workers in the field and those around them only further enhance the likelihood of continued disconnect between aid programming and the needs or desires of those on the ground.

Domestic workers, who are vulnerable to suspicion and accusations of theft, are also unlikely to feel comfortable being transparent and at ease with their employers, as their livelihood depends on a positive recommendation from the employer once he or she inevitably departs for a new post. Domestic staff must find ways of managing employers' narrow and changeable boundaries of intimacy, performing the correct amount of closeness and distance, as well as displaying acts of scrupulous trustworthiness, to overcome an inherent mistrust that aid workers feel about their own vulnerability to Senegalese more broadly. Though stolen TVs or damaged bike tires are unlikely to interfere with aid workers' ability to support their families, for domestic workers, losing the trust of an employer could mean termination followed by a long period of unemployability.

3 | STRATIGRAPHIES OF MOBILITY

TAMARA, A THIRTY-FOUR-YEAR-OLD MOTHER OF two from the Balkans, said the affordable domestic care that living in Africa guaranteed was not only part of her decision to return to a position in the field but "the biggest part" of that decision. She was tired of working a full shift at her NGO's headquarters in the United States and a full shift at home, she told me over a coffee at Café Layu, a fashionable American-style coffee shop across from a UN office and next to a French supermarket. Around us sat other professional people with laptops or in groups of two or three, drinking lattes and eating banana bread. I caught snippets of conversation in non-native English about "impact assessments" and "community action plans" from neighboring tables. Tamara told me that her husband, who had been the primary caregiver to their two young children while she worked, was tired of life in the US as well. She explained that they were barely scraping by on her single income. "You know, between that and feeling like we never actually had time to do anything because you're either working or you're preparing all the things to be able to go to work, I don't know, I felt like America was really difficult for families . . . so we went back overseas. I'm like, 'Well, at least we'll get a nanny. And that will be nice.'"

Tamara now employs not only a live-in nanny and housekeeper but a security guard and a part-time gardener as well. She is still the sole breadwinner for her family, but they live much more comfortably on her salary in Dakar. Instead of the cramped apartment that they rented in Maryland, they have a large house just a few blocks from the beach, with a separate structure on the property for the housekeeper's living quarters. Tamara takes taxis to and from work, where she coordinates her NGO's program to prevent irregular migration through the Sahel. She comes home to a clean house, washed and ironed laundry, children picked up from school and bathed, and sits down to a meal shopped for and cooked by her housekeeper/nanny.

The story of Senegal and migration that is most commonly told— indeed, the subject of my first book (Hannaford 2017)—is the same one that Tamara's job targets: that of Senegalese traveling out. To Europe by plane, by pirogue, over the Sahara Desert; using their religious networks, sending home remittances, drowning in the Mediterranean Sea. In this chapter, however, I seek to explore the role of migration in this story of expatriate aid workers and their domestic workers. There are two stories of economic migration here—that of aid workers finding remunerative careers and enhanced lifestyles through North-South migration and that of rural Senegalese women coming to the city to find precarious employment as domestic workers. By putting them into conversation, I hope to highlight the interdependence of these two migration stories and the inexorable inequities of mobility they reflect. The migration of aid workers to Senegal gives them the means for increased status, financial well-being, and an enhanced work and family balance. The migration of rural Senegalese women to Dakar to work as their domestics can also provide some financial gain but just as often leaves domestic workers mired in economic and social precarity and separated from family.

EXPATS QUA EXPATS

There are relatively few studies that treat expats to Africa as economic migrants.[1] Indeed they are regularly ignored or overlooked in conversations about global migration. Though the factors pushing and pulling those engaging in "privileged migration" may differ from those that we traditionally call migrants (generally those from the Global South), I argue that these development workers have moved from one place to another for work opportunities and an improved quality of life and are thus, in essence, economic migrants.[2] That we usually fail to include expats in the category of economic migrants—that there are so few studies of them, even by organizations that track migration closely, like the IOM and the OECD—says a great deal about our understanding of whose mobility should be controlled and disciplined and who should be allowed unfettered access to mobility.[3] To wit, it is very difficult to get clear numbers of expats residing in Senegal, or in Africa more broadly. Organizations like the IOM do not have useful data on the matter. Researchers do seem to agree, however, that it is probable that there are more Western expatriates in Africa today employed by development agencies than there were at any point in the colonial period (Stirrat 2000, 33).

The term *expat* is a notoriously vague one, with different meanings in different contexts and at different times. In corporate literature it tends to describe highly skilled laborers sent overseas for a determined amount of time to do a particular job. In previous iterations, it has meant someone who has left their country definitively, never again to return. Today it can also refer to migrant pensioners, who leave not for work but because they are no longer tied to any location by their employment.[4] Van Bochove and Engbersen (2013) identify two common characterizations of expatriates in academic literature. Expats—whom they define as "highly skilled temporary migrants and accompanying spouses"—are either described as being adventure loving and endlessly curious globetrotters or parochial cosmopolitans who want to associate only with those in their bubble and live a life as close to that at home as possible.[5] Leonard (2010) has sought to make distinctions within the category of expatriate, arguing that nation, gender, and class stratifications make the category much less cohesive than generally presented.

Nevertheless, moving from one part of the world to another explicitly in search of work that allows for a better quality of living is economic migration. Though race and colonial legacy often prevent scholars, governments, and laypeople from categorizing expatriates from the West to the developing world in this manner, their transnationalism is a constitutive part of postcolonial mobility that merits analytical attention.

DAKAR AS AN EXPAT HAVEN

Dakar is an attractive destination for economic migrants from the Global North. The low cost of living, relatively high quality of life for those with means, and the informality of the job market make Dakar a desirable place for relocation for many Europeans and Americans in search of a good life in an era of growing inequality everywhere.

This relates to a broader trend of Western movement to the Global South to take advantage of wealth disparity. New labor patterns include the "human cloud," where white collar jobs are divided into discrete tasks or projects and then put into the ether for workers who can be anywhere as long as they have access to the internet connection (Mottola and Coatney 2021). For so-called digital nomads, the developing world is a good place to be because of its relative high quality of life for low cost. Destinations like Bali are attracting increasing numbers of freelancers, contract workers, and other members of the global gig economy.[6]

Similarly, this era has seen a rise in people from high-income countries moving to low-income countries for retirement, in what has been called international retirement migration.[7] A French pension goes a great deal further in Tangiers than it does in Lyon, and Morocco offers pensioners considerably more status than they would enjoy at home, not to mention a gentler climate. Though this phenomenon is not entirely new—Spanish beaches have swarmed with retired Northern Europeans since the 1950s, and San Miguel de Allende, Mexico, has played host to American retirees since the 1930s—the geographic scale of this phenomenon is expanding. Some developing countries are encouraging this; Costa Rica, Panama, Mexico, Malaysia, and Nicaragua provide a simple residency process, *pensionado* visas, and tax breaks for foreign income. With the ability to FaceTime or Zoom with grandchildren; read, watch, and listen to the news of home in real time; and stay virtually on top of banking and other aspects of life administration, almost no corner of the world feels too remote.

Postcolonial Africa offers expats several things that make it an appealing destination—including a relatively low cost of living, unique amenities,[8] and—for white expats—the prestige of being white in a postcolonial context with enduring white supremacy. Notably for my research, many expat jobseekers find that prestige to be extremely useful in acquiring employment, including in the humanitarian/development sector. As Barbara Harrel-Bond put it, "During an emergency, whatever their background, almost any white face which arrives on the scene [in Africa] has the chance of a job" (quoted in Hancock 1989, 8). Several of my expat interlocutors had arrived in Dakar after frustrating struggles to find steady employment and a sustainable lifestyle in Europe or the United States. In Dakar they quickly gained a foothold in the local economy and enjoyed status— and amenities like copious, affordable domestic help—that they could not have hoped to possess at home.[9]

Laurel, a thirty-year-old American woman working in development in Dakar, had trouble finding work in the nonprofit sector at home in Portland, Oregon. She searched for a job for over two years, supporting herself by working in an unrelated business run by a family friend. After that job ended, she was finally offered a position in community development, but it was in Seattle, hours away, and it was only half-time. With an unemployed husband and a young son to support, she couldn't afford to take the job. Her husband, who was Senegalese and also struggling to find work in the US, suggested they move to Dakar and she agreed. "I really needed a change," she said. "I was unemployed. I was collecting unemployment and that could not last long. And I was also having a really hard time finding work."

Within two months of arriving in Dakar, Laurel not only found a job in development but a much more significant position than those she had been applying for the in the US. She became the director of the Senegal country office of an international NGO, despite having no experience in a leadership position. It was a brand-new office, and Laurel was tasked with finding office space, setting up the office, hiring the staff, and running operations in Dakar. These are all tasks that she had never performed, and though there was some training from the NGO, as an American, she was mostly assumed to be able to learn the skills on the job. Her salary was enough to support her whole family, pay for rent, a maid, and a nanny, as her husband pursued his dream of making it in the Senegalese music industry.

So-called trailing spouses of expat development workers who are from the West can take advantage of their position of privilege in the job market in this same way. I met many trailing spouses who had moved to Dakar for their spouse's job in the development industry, only to find work in it themselves when at the post. Many trailing spouses are hired by international NGOs on "local salary," without the amenities and inflation of expat packages that they do not require, as their spouse already usually has such a package. They compete favorably with actual locals for these "local" positions, ensuring that even more of the budgets of organizations targeting development in Senegal end up in non-Senegalese pockets.

Outside the aid industry, I saw this same story repeat among expats I met in Dakar. Marco and Tommaso, friends and young architects from the south of Italy, both failed to obtain a job in Italy upon graduating from architecture school and even struggled to find an unpaid internship, which was the common path for most of their fellow graduates. They blamed a combination of nepotism and the economic crisis for their inability to find work. Finally, they decided to try Dakar, which they had heard was rapidly developing and thus in need of architects. Within their first week in Dakar, they each had several interviews and a job offer. Now employed with separate employers in Senegal, they credited the openness and vitality of Dakar's economy for this access, though they were both aware that being white Westerners was a huge asset in penetrating Dakar's job market. Though by Italian standards they were still quite young and inexperienced, in Senegal, their prestige as Europeans and the relative lack of competitors for highly skilled positions made them desirable hires. Their educational and racial capital gave them an automatic boost in the job market.

Rhacel Parreñas discusses a phenomenon called "contradictory class mobility" in her study of Filipina migrant domestic workers. The term refers to the "simultaneous experience of upward and downward mobility in migration" (2001b, 150). Filipina domestic and healthcare workers move from the Philippines to places like Italy and the US to make more money than they ever would in the Philippines; however, their occupational status actually decreases as they enter the low-status field of domestic work. Many Filipina domestic workers possess college degrees or other kinds of training, but what Parreñas calls collectively "the nation-based hierarchy of educational qualifications, the devalued accreditation of degrees from the Third World, and the limits of mobility in the Philippines" conspire to make Filipina migrants downwardly mobile in terms of career status. The contradiction is that their class status improves in the Philippines through this same migration; as migrant women, they are able to send money home to support family at a level that would have been impossible had they stayed home.

In the case of the expatriate labor migrants in Senegal like Laurel, Marco, and Tommaso, who moved in the opposite direction, from

Europe and the US to the developing world, the class mobility is equally contradictory. Expats—particularly but not exclusively white Western expats—occupy an elite status in Africa with privilege, access, and authority that would have been hard to achieve at home. Their class mobility is supercharged by moving downward in the so-called hierarchy of nations. This allows them to pursue an accelerated career track and as well as an elevated lifestyle.[10]

Like so many aspects of this study, this phenomenon has echoes in Senegal's colonial past. In the so-called development period which began after WWII, in the decades before Senegal's independence from France in 1960, there was a marked increase in European migrants to Senegal. These migrants, unlike earlier migrant flows from the metropole, were coming to fill mid-tier administrative jobs. When they arrived in Dakar, these European workers competed with an emerging class of educated Senegalese who had capitalized on the French colonial opportunities to study both at home and in France. Kept out of the higher ranks of professions by racial barriers, they soon found themselves pushed out of mid- and lower-level jobs in both industry and government because of the lower-class Europeans who were arriving to take those positions (Mercier 1965, 173). A growing group of Senegalese elites found themselves superfluous in a system that would not allow them into upper ranks and increasingly squeezed them out of middle and lower ranks as well. European migrants were a direct obstacle to their employment and advancement. The tensions created by this competition led to the movements that later solidified into independence.

There was even a newer class of migrant coming to fill working class jobs in Senegal in the postwar period, the *petit blanc*, or lower-class white person; as conditions in Europe became more difficult for these artisans and laborers, Senegal seemed like a good place for a low-skilled worker to try to make a living. A French person with even just a primary school education could access a decent salary (Cruise O'Brien 1972, 66). The development era itself meant there were new opportunities for workers and, there, they found that they could live at a higher level than they could in the postwar metropole (Mercier 1955, 146). Thus, as the upper ranks were seeing a limited but novel "Senegalization," the subordinate ranks were seeing an increased "Europeanization" (136). These new migrants were not intending to stay or settle in Senegal but were merely there to make money to advance their interests and their futures back home in the metropole.[11] They did so at the expense of local people who the development and investment initiatives were ostensibly supposed to uplift.[12]

As Paul Mercier noted at the time, "For the great majority of the European population, *la vie coloniale* represents a promotion compared to metropolitan life: with the same qualifications and social origins, one can enjoy a more favorable material situation, more easily attainable positions of authority or management, and a kind of life made for only the most privileged classes in the metropole" (1955, 136, my translation).[13] Decades later, my aid worker interlocutors who came to Senegal looking for work found the same kind of promotion and perks as they filled the ranks of NGOs in Senegal and throughout the developing world.

LEANING IN

Expat aid workers like Tamara spoke in interviews about how access to copious and affordable domestic labor in Senegal and other posts in the developing world allowed them to lean in at work and strike the elusive balance between work and family life. The development workers I spoke to in Dakar expressed the common complaints of middle-class professionals: working weekends, staying late when under deadlines, and work problems following them into their off-work hours. Being overseas, these workers did not have help from extended family in childcare, but being in Senegal afforded them another opportunity to achieve a healthier work-life balance: namely, through affordable domestic labor. Though women in development work face some of the same kinds of discrimination, lack of promotion, and harassment as women and nonbinary workers in other fields (Humanitarian Women's Network 2016), an overseas post was cited by many women I interviewed as an opportunity to pursue their career without sacrificing time with their family in ways unthinkable while working at HQ.[14]

After serving in the Peace Corps, getting a master's degree in policy, and working for a development contractor in Washington, DC, Gemma joined USAID where, at forty-six, she held a supervisory role. When we spoke, she was bound for an even more senior position at another international post, and she expressed pride and ambition about her trajectory. Gemma compared her experience to that of a girlfriend in Washington, DC, who had stayed at the development contractor where Gemma had worked before joining USAID. This friend was advancing much more slowly at her agency, and when she finally got an opportunity for a director position, she turned it down. Gemma thought her friend was crazy for refusing this major promotion. Gemma, who is a mother of two, framed her friend's decision thusly: "It's one of those things where she has a family now, and she's trying to find work-life balance."

Before they moved abroad, Gemma, too, struggled to balance the demands of work and family. For the first ten years of their marriage in Washington, DC, when Gemma worked full-time at the private development agency and later for USAID's domestic office, she and her husband could not afford childcare or household help. In this period, Gemma's husband cared for the children during the day and worked nights as a parking valet. She recounts literally passing their first child back and forth to cover their childcare needs: "There were times when he would drive downtown, pass the kid to me. I would take the kid, get back on the metro, and go home for him to be on time and for me to leave on time." This "tag-team parenting" has become more common in the US, as parents embrace working different schedules as a means to reduce childcare costs (Bianchi 2011, 18). Gemma and her husband never had the time or money for vacations, let alone the cost of daycare in DC, which can be upward of $2,000 a month per child. Gemma recalled coming home from her demanding and stressful job, strapping her infant onto her back, and cooking for the family, starting the laundry, bathing the children, and putting them to bed on her own while her husband worked his night job.

When Gemma took her first overseas post with USAID and the family moved to East Africa, she and her husband hired a nanny, a housekeeper, and a chauffeur. Right away her work and her home life changed dramatically. With the help of her domestic staff, she was able to continue to lean in at work while enjoying her personal time as well. When she returned home from work, the house would be clean; the laundry would be washed, folded, and put away; the dinner hot and ready to eat; and the kids bathed and ready for bed. This meant that she could finally spend time with the husband who for so many years of tag-team parenting she had seen only in passing. When "we first started being home together at night, we were like, 'Oh, who are you?'" Gemma recalled, laughing. "We didn't even know how to act with each other. We hadn't been home together at night." Overall, Gemma said, their quality of life had improved tenfold since moving to the developing world, as they were able to afford relief from their household's care burden. "It's just allowed us to, like, have leisure time and think about exercising regularly and getting together with friends. And obviously we spend much more time with our kids and with each other and friends."

In Dakar, Gemma employed a gardener named Ibou and a house-keeper named Sokhna, who also took care of the children. In addition to cleaning the house and doing the laundry, Sokhna cooked on weeknights and did the grocery shopping. She was there to receive deliveries and supervise maintenance to the house when Gemma and her husband were at work. She also walked the youngest daughter to school and was present to watch both girls when they returned home after school. Gemma said she was particularly grateful they had had a few years of child-rearing on their own in the US so they could fully appreciate the help.

Gemma's family's location overseas benefitted them in other material ways as well. Gemma and her husband paid the mortgage for their home in a DC suburb by having renters, and because they lived rent-free abroad through her job, they were able to save much more than they could have at home. She said, "That's another huge thing to being overseas. Because our expenses have gone down, because your housing is taken care of . . . I've been able to pay back loans, and we've actually been able to save some money. When you're not overseas, it's so hard. So hard."

She noted that although they loved the neighborhood of their home in Maryland, the school district was not ideal. However, while abroad, her job paid for her children to be in elite international schools, so that was not a concern. As a US foreign service employee, she was eligible for retirement at fifty if she had twenty years of service behind her. Though she didn't think she would stop working yet, the material security of knowing that she could allowed her to make career and family choices for reasons other than purely financial ones.

MIGRANT DOMESTIC WORKERS

Gemma's nanny, Sokha, like Gemma, migrated to Dakar for an employment opportunity, as did many of the nannies and maids I interviewed for this project. A 2010 study that surveyed 102 domestic workers in Dakar found only six respondents had actually been born in the city (Barnett 2011). Known alternately as *janq* (the Wolof word for virgin, generally used to mean a young female), *petite bonne* (the French word for maid), *mbindaan* (Wolof for servant), or *fatou* (a generic Senegalese girl's name),[15] domestic workers for Senegalese families in Dakar most commonly migrate from the rural regions of Fatick, Kaolack, Diourbel, and Thiès (Africa, Caribbean and Pacific Observatory on Migration 2012, 4),[16] though a smaller number migrate from neighboring nations (Ndari 2018, 39; Bop 2010).

Women in rural Senegal are motivated to leave school and are drawn into urban migration as domestic workers because of environmental, economic, and social conditions that have left villages at a loss to provide a promising life to young people, and thus many villagers look to Dakar (and beyond) to make their way in the world.[17] Though this kind of migration from village to city was long a seasonal cycle of migration,[18] as urbanization takes hold in Senegal just as in other places in Africa, many have abandoned the rural lifestyle, and rural-to-urban has become a more permanent migration, including for domestic workers.[19] The fallout of colonial exploitation, ruinous postcolonial economic policy imposed by the International Monetary Fund (IMF) and the World Bank, and environmental problems such as drought and overfishing have made rural Senegal a place of exodus.[20]

In the 1980s, Senegal was one of the first African countries to agree to structural adjustment policies in exchange for loans from the World Bank and the IMF. Through these policies, the IMF and the World Bank pushed the Senegalese government to shrink government, withdraw many of its social services, abolish trade barriers, and privatize its markets.[21] These programs had a profound effect on Senegal's agricultural sector, abolishing agricultural cooperatives that small farmers relied on for purchasing the provisions needed to farm cash crops. Without these cooperatives, the majority of small farmers could no longer depend on farming for financial gain (Perry 1997, 212). These changes, combined with a series of severe droughts in the 1970s and 1980s and the subsequent crisis in groundnut cultivation, solidified the decline of the agricultural sector as a viable livelihood for many.

The historical processes that have valued rural women's domestic labor cheaply[22] are to the benefit of Dakar families, who are also undergoing social changes. As more women in urban areas move into formal employment and more urban girls attend and remain longer in school, the erstwhile free domestic labor done by young urban women in the house is now increasingly done for (low) pay by rural transplants who have found that the domestic labor that they were doing for free in their households in the village can be a source of income in the city.[23] This pull factor has meant that there are more female minors than male minors among rural-to-urban migrants in Dakar (Bop 2010, 1). A survey of 540 minors working as maids by the NGO Enda Tiers Monde in 1996 found that 56 percent had chosen the work to meet their own needs and provide for their families in their village of origin, whereas 43 percent reported they had been forced by their family to take up this work. Notably, only 8 percent reported being happy with their work (Understanding Children's Work 2010).

Awa, now a nanny and housekeeper for an American aid worker family, was among this group of girls who came to Dakar from a Serer village near Thies, hoping to find a way to support herself and send money home to her family. At just fifteen years old, her first job was as a maid for a Wolof family, and she was not one of the 8 percent who found happiness in her employment. She eventually left the job for the same reason that many other girls and women leave: the long hours, low wages, and poor treatment that characterize domestic work. Though there are laws governing domestic work in Senegal, as in other contexts, the work is informal and escapes official regulation and is thus ripe for exploitation.[24] Turnover is incredibly high in this sector as quitting is the most effective tool domestic workers possess to have agency in dynamics with employers.

Awa, now in her late thirties, was renting a room in a crowded compound of concrete huts in a *quartier populaire* of Dakar. Her husband and two of her three children lived in the Serer village outside Thies from which she hailed. I joined her in her rented room one evening after she got home from a day of work as a maid and nanny for expat aid workers in the Almadies. As I sat down on the only piece of furniture in her concrete hut, a single, thin foam mattress on the floor, the power went out. Power cuts are frequent in Dakar, and although development workers like Awa's employer and other expats have generators that keep their offices and homes running during the cuts, in Awa's hut I could no longer see my hand in front of my face. I heard her feeling around for something, and then a few clicks. She called out to her daughter, who was playing with some other girls and boys in the pitch-black courtyard outside her hut, handed her a few coins, and sent her to get batteries for the flashlight from a local corner store. My eyes had adjusted by the time she came back, and I watched as Awa expertly replaced the large batteries in the large yellow camping flashlight and clicked it on to illuminate the room.

Awa explained to me that after she left her first job, she had worked for other households in Dakar, going back and forth between Dakar and her village to marry and bear three children with a man there. Two years prior to our meeting, a friend who was working for an American family offered to help place her with an American family as well. She was told the conditions and the pay were better with toubab (white) employers, and she jumped at the chance to elevate herself. "You know," she told me matter-of-factly, "working people, they want to advance." Just as for Gemma, who was about to move from Dakar to Southeast Asia for a higher position in the ranks of USAID, for Awa, the switch from a local family to an expat family was a promotion that came with better conditions and a raise.

Awa's friend found her the position she now held, caring five days a week for a newborn and a toddler and cleaning the home of an employee of USAID and his stay-at-home wife. Awa made about $220 a month, a great deal more than she had previously made with a local Lebanese family,[25] even after working for them for over twenty years. With this sum, she was able to send money back to support her husband and older children, as well as rent the little unfurnished room for herself and her daughter in Dakar. She told me frankly that she did not like living apart from the rest of her family, but she knew her wages would not support the whole family in pricey Dakar.

For domestic workers, most of the pleasures of Dakar that expats enjoy are far out of reach. Many domestic workers live precariously in Dakar, where cost of living has risen steadily.[26] Women can usually recount with remarkable accuracy what the previous four or five prices for daily-purchase items such as oil, rice, bread, and milk have been, when they changed, and in what increments. Economists have shown that the price of goods and services in sub-Saharan countries can be 25–28 percent higher than in comparable countries elsewhere. Food items, they found, are even 35 percent more expensive in African cities, making the cost of living particularly unmanageable for low-income households (Nakamura et al. 2019). Stretching a weekly budget to cover the necessary costs to house and feed a family with these increases becomes a process of intricate calculations, juggling, and resourcefulness. For many rural-to-urban migrants like Awa, it simply doesn't make sense to try to have her whole family live with her in Dakar.

Living apart from their children is a fact of life for many domestic workers in the global economy.[27] As more middle-class women have moved into the workforce across the world, the reproductive labor that women have traditionally done for free (cooking, cleaning, elder care, childcare) has been become a purchasable commodity. When this domestic labor goes on the marketplace, it gets valued quite low, and families in the US, Europe, Asia, and the Middle East look for cheap sources of this labor, thus creating a demand for migrant women.[28] This is the dynamic known as the international division of reproductive labor (Parreñas 2001b). These migrant women, in turn, often leave their own loved ones behind in the care of poorer, usually rural women from their own nation, as captured by Arlie Hochschild's term "the global care chain" (2003).

Like other employers of domestic workers, expat development workers as a class are dependent on the reproductive labor of a portion of the global lower class for the reproduction of their own status. In the scenario of aid workers in the developing world, it is the affordable domestic labor reserve in these countries that allows these privileged migrants to bring their children with them as they change countries for work. The "servants of globalization" (Parreñas 2001b) here are generally the same demographic: the black and brown women of poorer countries. Like Awa, many of these women have rearranged their domestic lives to be able to work in the development workers' domestic lives, including leaving their children with family in rural areas when they migrate to the city. This sacrifice puts them alongside the domestic workers studied elsewhere in the world, who parent from afar while caring for and nurturing the children of other, richer families.[29]

Tamara's housekeeper, Caroline, became an international migrant when she migrated with Tamara's family to Senegal. Tamara had hired Caroline to be her nanny when she was posted in Niamey, Niger. When Tamara got a new post in Dakar, she assumed she would be saying goodbye to Caroline and the other woman she employed in Niamey, a full-time housekeeper and cleaner. She was surprised that when she announced their upcoming departure, Caroline said she wanted to come with them. "I was kind of taken aback initially," Tamara recalled. "I think I had said something like 'I would never dare to ask you, but if it was up to me, I would keep you forever,' you know. Just kind of like that. A very friendly . . . but I never assumed." Tamara said it hadn't crossed her mind that she could bring Caroline, despite the fact that Tamara's children were very attached to her, because Caroline had a daughter in Niger. But Caroline, a widow, had already separated from her daughter to come from the village to Niamey to earn money to support her by caring for Tamara's children. Like Awa, Caroline had opted for rural-to-urban migration for domestic work to have the means to support her daughter from afar. Tamara says she had been doubtful and expressed guilt about internationally separating mother and daughter but that Caroline had insisted. "My nanny made me understand this is not something she was doing with us; this was something she was already doing. If it wasn't with us, it would be with someone else."

Fosterage, or children being raised by family members other than the biological mother and father, has a long tradition in West Africa and is not unique to the contemporary period of migration.[30] It is not a stigmatized practice, and it is likely that Caroline's family found her actions to be a reasonable parenting strategy, prioritizing her financial support of her daughter over her physical co-presence. In a context where material well-being is not easily attained, families have been forced to practice their kinship flexibly. Increasingly, in recent years, in response to the demands of neoliberal globalization, they have also had to practice kinship transnationally (Hannaford 2017, 6). This perspective on the structural issues framing Caroline's decision to leave her daughter behind made Tamara feel less personally guilty about the arrangement, viewing herself not as the root cause of Caroline's separation from her daughter, but merely the beneficiary.

DOMESTIC WORK FOR INTERNATIONAL MIGRATION

Awa's friend Ndeye joined us in Awa's little room, coming straight from her work as a nanny and maid, although it was after nine o'clock. She explained she didn't always stay so late, but that her employer, who worked for an American development organization, was out to dinner with friends. The employer's husband lived and worked in the US and visited only every few months. Ndeye's employer was able to single-parent their two-and-a-half-year-old child while pursuing her career and maintaining an active social life with friends because Ndeye took care of the child Monday to Friday and on occasional weekends and evenings when needed.

As the flashlight made shadow patterns on the ceiling, Ndeye and Awa discussed how much easier it was to work for toubabs than Senegalese families. Like Awa, Ndeye too, worked for a Senegalese family after migrating to Dakar—in her case, from the Casamance, in the south of Senegal. Her job with a Wolof family was Monday to Saturday, which included sleeping at their home, and she explained that she was never off the clock. Now, the work itself was easier, since expat households have things like washers and dryers and vacuum cleaners that make the work of housekeeping much less onerous. Awa exclaimed that she had become so unused to traditional laundering by hand that her hands became raw and sore when she washed her own clothing that way.

Ndeye had gotten her first job with an American family by way of a friend who was working for them. Her friend had been two years with the family when a previous employer offered to bring her to the US to work for the employer there. Her friend asked Ndeye to take over her current job so that she could migrate overseas. All the domestic workers I spoke to were aware of the possibility of employment for an expatriate family leading to international migration and this was widely considered another advantage of the job.

As I have argued elsewhere, contemporary Senegal is characterized by a "culture of migration" in which international mobility is imbued with prestige. Interrupted pathways to financial security and social status push Senegalese men and women to look outside Senegal (*bitim rëw)* for opportunities to build successful social lives within Senegal. Nonmigrants see the evidence of migrants' successes in the form of new housing construction, remittances to family, and acclaim from the government, and thus the world outside Senegal is imagined as a place of limitless wealth and reward. This culture of migration not only encourages emigration as a pathway to success and social status but also promotes myths and notions of success that in turn shape the everyday behavior of those who never leave. This culture of migration has troubled earlier conceptions of class, desirability, and honor within Senegal, which serves to further stimulate migration and dreams of migration.[31]

When I asked Ndeye if she would like to do what her friend has done and move to the US with her employers, she let out an emphatic "Waaw waaw!" (Yes indeed!) and continued: "Travel? Go to America? Of course I want to. As soon as I find someone who'll bring me with them, I'll go!" Awa and I laughed at her enthusiastic response, but nearly all the domestic workers I spoke to gave a version of the same answer. Most held a steadfast, if vague idea that to become an *immigré*, to join the ranks of Senegalese who live overseas, would mean access to a new kind of status and the potential to advance their own and their families' fortunes.

Marie Claude was equally emphatic when I asked her about the possibility of migration. At just twenty-six years old, she was living apart from her ten-year-old son, who lived with his paternal grandparents in a coastal town called Fatick. Marie Claude had left school after getting pregnant as a teenager. She eventually left her son with his grandparents so that she could move to Dakar and work as a maid and a cook for expats. A friend who was already working for an American family put Marie Claude in touch with her first employer, an American diplomat, who was supposed to be posted in Senegal for three years. When he left after only six months, Marie Claude was unexpectedly out of work. As the first chapter made clear, being employed by a professional class who moves so frequently makes domestic work for expats profoundly unstable and precarious. Luckily, Marie Claude eventually found another position with an American aid worker in her fifties, who was single with no children of her own.

Marie Claude showed me pictures of her son Paul as I sat with her in the rented bedroom that she shared with a cousin in a half-constructed apartment building in Parcelles, a banlieue of Dakar. We sat on the heavy wooden double bed she shared with her cousin in a room that fit little else besides an overstuffed wardrobe and a small desk cluttered with beauty products and other items. The building, like many others on the sandy street, was not complete. The concrete staircase was unfinished and had no railing and continued past Marie Claude's second-floor bedroom to an as-yet-unbuilt third floor. Such unfinished buildings are common across Senegal, as their owners await the funds to complete them (Melley 2010). Parcelles is a neighborhood where many overseas migrants have invested in home construction, including Marie Claude's landlord, using their earnings in Europe to slowly build a concrete foundation and future in Senegal.

Marie Claude's son Paul would visit for summer holidays but during the year her visits with him were few and far between. She was, however, going to see him in a few weeks, she told me, for the occasion of his communion. Her boss had permitted her to take some time off and go down to Fatick, and she was looking forward to the celebration. Our conversation that afternoon was frequently interrupted by phone calls from family, a visit from the tailor who was making Marie Claude and her cousin outfits for an upcoming family wedding, and various other distractions. Despite it being a weekday, Marie Claude was not at work because her boss was traveling out of the country for work.

When I asked about her boss of three years, Marie Claude did not hesitate to sing her praises, thanking God as she told me she worked for a very good woman. "If Americans were all like her, Senegalese would never say a bad word about them," she gushed. Marie Claude began to list the things about her boss that made her such a good employer, mostly how easygoing and reasonable she was. "I have never seen her angry," she told me. "When I started, she told me straightaway, 'I don't get angry.' I have never seen her make a face at me or tell me what I'm doing is bad. Never. I swear. She is not demanding. I've never asked her permission for something and had her say no. If she travels for a month, she tells me don't come to work. If she travels three months, she tells me don't come to work but she pays me my salary."

Marie Claude was satisfied in her work, which she said was much better than work in the restaurant industry for which she trained. "You're not exhausted, you have free time, you are at ease." In addition to the cooking and the cleaning, she did all the grocery shopping for her employer. She had learned to make many American dishes as well as some Mexican specialties for her boss, a native Texan who enjoyed spicy food. She was glad to be learning English and practicing with her employer, who spoke only a bit of French. We agreed that she was lucky her job did not include caring for children, as that is so much work, though she said that she would learn English more quickly if she were with children all day.

Despite her overall satisfaction in her job, when I asked about the future, Marie Claude said she would jump at any chance to leave Senegal. "Ah, Senegal—it's no good here." When I protested that Senegal is *neex*, the Wolof word for enjoyable or nice, she conceded, "It's *neex*, but there's no money." When I pushed back again and said that there was evidence of lots of money in Senegal, that there were rich Senegalese people living and going out near where she worked, she countered, "The money here only goes to one side. It's not for everyone, and it's very hard for us." Marie Claude didn't see Senegal as a place that offered her a financial future. She imagined America would have more opportunities than Senegal, which she viewed as a place of inequity, of inaccessible wealth that only went to "one side." Though she loved the lush tropical region of the Casamance where she grew up and where her parents still lived, and agreed that it was much nicer than Dakar, she saw no possibility for maintaining a livelihood there either—the work there depended entirely on the seasonality of the tourist industry. For six months a year, everything was closed and, as she told me, "You can't stay there the other six months."

I asked Marie Claude about the changes that the development industry had brought to the Casamance, and she told me there had been many "*projets toubabs*"[32] there: a nursery school, a maternity hospital. None of these projects, however, had made the Casamance a viable place for her to build a sustainable financial future. When I asked about what kinds of *projets toubabs* her boss was involved in, Marie Claude had no information on the subject. Like nearly all the domestic workers I spoke to, she had never inquired or been told about her boss's development work. For Marie Claude, it was entirely irrelevant to her life. The only way the development industry had directly impacted her life was by providing the opportunity to cook and clean for an American expat in Dakar.

It is not surprising that Marie Claude didn't believe in the development industry's power to change the circumstances of her life through its programming. James Ferguson, too, has noted that increasingly, African citizens have moved away from belief in a modernity-focused, just-wait-and-you'll-get-there approach to developmentalism, which may once have given them hope for the future in their country. Increasingly, it is migration out of Africa that seems to promise a pathway to social and financial success. "Not progress, then, but egress," as Ferguson concludes (2006, 192).

Marie Claude lit up when I asked her about her boss's home. When I asked about the amenities, she told me it had "everything!" Air conditioning, a vacuum cleaner, a washing machine where Marie Claude washed her own clothes as well. Wide-eyed and with exaggerated movements, she described her boss's home as being "*impec*," short for the French *impeccable*, flawless or perfect. Spending her days amid the amenities of this American expat home was signaling to her much more about which places promised a good life than a maternity hospital or other *projets toubabs* in Senegal ever could. The truly meaningful life change she could anticipate from the development industry was not that it would transform her country, but that it would take her out of her country so that she might clean her American employer's floors in a better place.

BRINGING HELP HOME

Domestic workers are not wrong to imagine that working in expat homes might one day lead to migration. Bringing good staff along to a next post was a frequent topic of discussion for expat aid workers, particularly in the case of nannies who had grown an intimate attachment to the children. However, the process of doing so was not easy. Alma, a regional director of a faith-based international NGO hoped to bring her Senegalese nanny with her when she moved to her next post in Haiti but ultimately decided against it. "She doesn't have a passport and you have to go through the US. She would never get a US visa, she had never taken a plane before, she would have to go through . . . it was Dakar-Paris, Paris-São Paulo, São Paulo-Panama, Panama-Haiti. I was just like, 'It's too much.' It was not realistic." Alma and her husband also calculated that it might have been more of a burden than a help to uproot the nanny and move her to a context where she didn't speak the language or have any local expertise or knowledge. Plus, if anything were to happen to her or she were to fall ill, they would be wholly responsible for her.

Bringing Senegalese domestic staff to the US or Europe was generally even more complicated than bringing them to another post in developing world, due to visa issues and labor laws. Ndeye's employer Kim's contract in Senegal was coming to an end when I spoke to her, and Kim would soon be working domestically for her employer in the US. Kim was contemplating bringing Ndeye home to work for her in the US at the end of her tour. The difficulty of obtaining a visa for her was only one of many obstacles in Kim's mind after meticulously investigating the law on these arrangements. She ticked off the legal responsibility for wages she would have if she sponsored Ndeye's visa to the United States as a domestic employee: "You have to pay the US minimum wage in that state. You have an eight-hour day and then you have to pay them overtime if they work on the weekends. And then you have to provide room and board, so that's not deducted. And then you have to provide an annual trip home, although I don't know if that's covered." The total she had come to, without the initial travel expenses, the annual trip home, or room and board, was about $1,600 a month—nearly five times what she currently pays Ndeye and for far fewer hours of care. When she compared this to the cost of daycare, which was upward of $2,000 per month in Los Angeles where she was relocating, however, this might make economic sense. Kim had not yet told Ndeye that she was weighing these options; she was confident that whenever she made a decision, Ndeye would agree to whatever she decided. Ndeye's future opportunity for international migration hung in the balance of Kim's personal calculations of what that care was worth to her and where she could get it for the most reasonable price.

The stark disparity in the affordability of care in the developing world versus at home becomes especially clear when aid workers contemplate returning to the US, making it difficult for expat development workers to opt to move home. Kim pointed out that many people get so dependent on the perks of working as an expat overseas in the developing world that they can no longer move home to work in their home country. "After a certain amount of years, you have kids. It's really hard to leave that lifestyle," she explained as she thought forward to life back in the United States. "I'm trying not to fall into that trap, but we'll see when I get back to the States what it's going to be like." She laughed, "After a couple of years I might be dying to go back *en mission* again." Kim, like Tamara, anticipated a time when she might decide that a work-life balance was possible for Western professional women only when they lived in the developing world.

For women like Marie Claude and Caroline and Awa, mobility is an imperative for financial viability and the economic support of loved ones, but that mobility comes at the expense of living with those loved ones. Furthermore, their mobility in country fails to offer them much more than mere subsistence and certainly guarantees very little in the way of long-term stability or transformational change in the circumstances of their life and the lives of those in their network.

The broader literature on the global care chain largely focuses on migration of women from the Global South to the Global North to work as care workers.[33] There is less work that looks at these global and transnational dynamics among care workers in the Global South, though this is where the majority of domestic workers are based.[34] There is a real dearth of literature on the topic in postcolonial Africa in particular.[35] In ignoring this population, we risk missing the broader dynamics that shape the labor opportunities and mobility of members of the "global precariat" (Standing 2011). A key difference in this domestic employment context is that, in contrast to the context where employers are citizens and domestic employees are migrants, the employers do not benefit from "citizenship privileges" over their employees in the way that, for example, US

employers of Latina immigrant maids or Taiwanese employers of In-
donesian migrants do. Here, the employees are usually citizens and
the employers are foreign migrants. However, the employers' status
as "expat" migrants trumps any privilege of citizenship that domestic workers hold. Citizenship of Senegal is not a privilege when
compared to expat privilege. When expat citizens of richer countries
can literally be airlifted out of the country in an emergency by their
embassy or agency, when their status as foreigners leads to more opportunities for career promotion and advancement, their migrant
status does not constitute precarity. That the employers are international migrants and the employees the local citizens ultimately does
little to upset the global social order of the international division
of reproductive labor, which gives care laborers so little control or
power over their financial or social future.[36] As in other contexts,
this iteration of the extraction of care perpetuates and capitalizes
upon global inequalities among women.

Migration in this scenario offers vastly different rewards to the
two groups that practice it. The expat workers use their migration
as a means to advantageous salaries, improved living conditions and
status, and affordable reproductive labor that makes possible their
working and family lives. For domestic workers, on the other hand,
engaging in urban migration to provide that reproductive labor often
means leaving family behind, living in conditions of poverty, and
gaining only a minimally improved chance of access to international
mobility.

Senegalese domestic workers display what is called "fractal precarity" (McIlwaine and Bunge 2019) not only because of their precarious
jobs[37] and their labor market immobility[38] but also their tangential
access to international mobility. As the next chapter shows, expat employers often perceive of their employment of domestic workers as
helping the domestic workers, or a win-win situation in which their
family receives care labor that they need and the domestic workers
earn money to support themselves and their families. Indeed, it is

framed as a win-win-win, as the employers are freed to do their development work, which, in theory, should benefit the communities of the domestic workers. In fact, however, as in most cases of domestic-worker migration scenarios, "the majority of the value accrues to the employers and their economies, rather than [the domestic workers] or their communities" (Silvey and Parreñas 2020, 3458).

4 | INEQUALITIES OF THE WORLD PERSONIFIED

RAYNA AND HER HUSBAND NEVER expected to have household help. "Like who are we to have staff? I grew up in a home that didn't have a lot of money. Greg came from probably a family that was a little more stable, but we didn't have maids or help!" she laughed. For Rayna, the only people who hired domestic servants were the ultra-wealthy—a category that did not fit with her self-identity as a crusader against poverty. But when they had their first child while she was posted as an aid worker in North Africa, they hired a nanny who also cleaned the house. When they had a second child and they moved to a post in Asia, they realized they needed two employees—a nanny and a housekeeper who could do the cooking. "I was like, 'Oh my god . . .'" Rayna covered her face in mock embarrassment. "And then here we have a housekeeper who cleans and cooks, we had a nanny, and then we had a driver! So, it worked out, but I was like, 'Oh my god, we have a driver. And a gardener. Oh my god, Greg, we have staff. What is going on?'" Though the couple had not grown up with domestic help nor ever expected to employ them, the affordability and banality of having domestic employees while an expat aid worker led Rayna and her husband to consider them a necessary part of their life abroad.

Expat aid workers often have ambivalent feelings about the domestic work they purchase and those who perform it. For aid worker employers, although they generally express relief and appreciation for the luxury of "having staff," they also feel embarrassment, guilt, and discomfort about hiring people to do their domestic labor and being the kind of people who "have staff." The inequities of race and nation that fuel their job opportunities are not only all around them in their overseas post but are brought directly into the home. As in other scenarios where expats hire local domestic staff, "global hierarchical structures are played out in the transnational household" (Lundström 2013, 45). Despite the bubbles of insulation separating aid workers and the general population that I discussed in chapter 2, the home becomes a transnational "contact zone" (Lundström 2013) where they cannot escape the realities of the wealth and opportunity gap between themselves and local people.

The "inequality and interdependency between developing and industrialized regions that are being perpetuated through the performance of domestic labor" (Wang 2013, 21) make aid workers react in particular ways to deflect, ease, or subvert the discomfort of sitting in their privilege. In this chapter, I explore three of these strategies. The first is to recast their employment of domestic workers as a duty, akin to the "white man's burden" that was used to legitimize colonial and subsequently development interventions. The second is to make a concerted effort to be a "good" or a "nice" boss; this can mean striving for emotional closeness with domestic staff, becoming preoccupied with how to share criticism or make requests for additional work and services, or going to great lengths to avoid firing them even when unhappy with the quality of their work. By fixating on details of "being a nice person," aid workers are able to deemphasize the power differential in their understandings of these relationships and avoid acknowledging the ethical structural issues that shape their employment of local people to work in their homes.

The third way that expat aid workers deal with their ambivalent feelings and discomfort about employing household help is to bring additional transactions into their relationship beyond paying them directly for domestic services. These include paying for additional training, supporting the workers' families financially, giving career and financial advice, and giving monetary and material gifts. Aid workers code these transactions as charitable,[1] in ways that help them avoid thinking of this extra investment as compensation for what they know are extremely low wages. Instead, using care as an idiom for these gestures of financial support puts them in the position not as exploiter of cheap labor but as benevolent patron or mentor. Thereby, this site of their exploitation of a labor reserve created by poverty can itself be reframed as their own efforts to "develop" or "aid" the poor.

WHAT EXPAT AID WORKERS DON'T LIKE

Self-aware cheek is a currency among aid workers online. Many a meme is posted and shared among aid workers that pokes fun at the absurdities of their work or the self-seriousness of their profession. This is an insider game—the same aid-worker Facebook groups that lampoon their own through silly memes and biting satire also passionately decry journalistic stories that they view as cherry-picking the worst cases of development incompetence or corruption and excoriate politicians who target development for criticism and drive down public support. Among aid workers, however, knowing winks and jabs at the profession build community and a sense of inclusion.[2]

A satirical website based on the popular Stuff White People Like, called Stuff Expat Aid Workers Like, launched in 2010 and still active as of 2021, is a good example of this self-mockery. Created and operated by expat aid workers (EAWs), it features tongue-in-cheek posts submitted by the EAW community confirming inside jokes that would be recognizable to all in the community. The comments sections on each post are mostly full of appreciation from fellow aid workers about the accuracy of the take. Items on the list include things that poke fun at how silly, slapdash, and unprofessional the field can be, like "#214 Writing their own job description" and "#135 Spiffy project names" to merciless takedowns of the absurdities of the expat lifestyle, including send-ups of how expat aid workers love bargaining for a local price ("stickin' it to the vendors and turning that per-diem into much-needed beer money"), dressing up in local garb ("giggles you hear are the locals' way of showing appreciation, and the stares are looks of true admiration"), and the local expat coffee shop ("the appeal of a big cup of coffee and a bagel for $10 will pull the EAW in every time"). The fond but wry portrait of the expat aid worker that emerges is of an earnest, well-meaning but staggeringly arrogant and myopic doofus (similar to the portrait that emerges on the original Stuff White People Like).

An October 2011 post entitled "#104 Feeling Ambivalent about 'the Help'" captures the familiar feeling of awkwardness that so many aid workers feel about their domestic staff.[3] Though it is obviously satire, the feelings described map so accurately onto the sentiments and concerns expressed by my expat aid worker interviewees that I quote it here in full:

> EAWs like (or at least often end up) feeling ambivalent about "the help." They think of themselves as scrappy and self-reliant—certainly more than capable of cooking, cleaning and washing clothes on their own. They also see all humanity as their brethren, nobody inherently more noble or deserving than the next. So, they are constitutionally predisposed to be uncomfortable with the subservient dynamic of house help.
>
> But they need help, don't they? Whether they are community-based or working from a swank office in a capital city, EAWs at least need the laundry done. And washing clothes by hand alone is a full time job. Part time at least. And they have that other full time job making the world right, so they feel justified in paying someone "the fair market rate" (which inconveniently hovers around the

global poverty line) to get some things done around the house. And they're doing their part to take a dent out of the always enormous national unemployment rate. Who can argue with that?

Who *needs* to argue with that? The EAW is in a constant state of arguing with herself over the whole endeavor.

Given her tidy salary and dank perks, she *could* pay more, but that's really distorting the local economy, and she's here to tread lightly so she can't go around doing that, can she? Or can she?

Anyway, she treats her 46-year-old "house girl" well. Much better than the locals. She pays her kids [*sic*] school fees, lets her leave for funerals and weddings and gives her the left-over . . . just about anything. She always thanks her profusely and insists on being called by her first name. She takes a certain pride in her munificence. But there's that gnawing question: Am I a saint or a sucker?

Most EAWs accept paying a small farang/mzungu/whatever[4] premium, but there's nothing an EAW loathes more than being taken for a ride. Paying a chump's rate for anything is a sure sign that you don't know the culture well enough to negotiate a local rate—a mistake an EAW cannot afford to make if he is to boast of any measure of field cred. Plus, EAWs are well versed in evils of dependency and paternalism, so there are limits to their largesse on principle.

But then there it is. Staring them right in the face and every day. The inequalities of the world personified in their hire.

A newbie who doesn't quite understand the delicate psychological equilibrium EAWs have constructed will, over $5 whiskeys, rudely compare the price of any of his petty indulgences with the monthly salary of the help. "You know, the costs of last night's stay at the Addis Sheraton would pay Muna's salary for 3 months." This is often followed by uncomfortable silence, far away looks or occasionally eye rolling. Then another gulp of whiskey.

Aid workers frequently expressed ambivalence about having domestic employees at all, not only because of the "inequalities of the world personified in their hire," but because help in the home required a breach of their intimate space. A few said that they put off hiring staff as long as possible, as they were uncomfortable with the idea of someone who was not family being in their home. A USAID employee named Ted and his wife delayed hiring house help when they moved to Dakar, due to "mostly just us feeling weird about having someone in the house." Once they found out they were going to have a baby, Ted and his wife hired a departing neighbor aid worker's housekeeper to come clean their sea-view apartment three days a week. "We got used to it pretty quickly," Ted said ruefully. "You come home and your house is clean." Ted insists, though, that they try to minimize the time their housekeeper works. "It's only a few hours. It's not . . . We don't. I mean there are other people that have their housekeepers around all the time. And . . . even when there's nothing to do, they're just there. Which seemed weird to us, so . . . We pay her the same, but she's only there for about three hours three times a week."

Other aid workers like Ted, particularly those without children, were eager to make their housekeeper and her labor less visible. Multiple people told me they shaped their housekeeper's hours so that they would not be home, leaving notes and money for the housekeeper and interacting in person as little as possible. Though they often framed this as being sure to be "out of her way" as she cleaned, it is also true that not witnessing the folding and ironing of your underclothes by a hired person goes some way toward avoiding the "moments of unease" (Fechter 2012, 1478) that aid workers feel about this dynamic. As Meredith, a consultant for the UN, put it, "It is really interesting how personal it is. It's not the same as the cleaners at work; you can feel bad for them, but you don't see them in your house; they are not touching your things." Having domestic workers in your home makes it impossible to hide from individual culpability in power and wealth inequalities. Meredith said that she often wondered what the housekeeper thought about her flexible schedule as a consultant working largely from home. "Even though it's weird, I wonder if she just thinks I don't do anything when I'm around the house." Meredith's unease at outsourcing her domestic work while she was home during the day made her project her moral misgivings onto the maid. "I'm uncomfortable," she said. "I wonder if she's judging me. It's me judging me."

Gwyneth, a British employee of a maternal and child health organization, also tried for her first few months to live without getting a housekeeper. "I'm quite protective of my space," she explained. Though her apartment is small, Gwyneth was finding that there were reasons why keeping an apartment in Senegal clean was different than doing so at home in England. Keeping a home clean and tidy in the coastal Sahelian climate involves vigilant dusting and mopping. Dakar is very dusty and humid; not keeping up with cleaning floors and surfaces means having a layer of dust and grime over everything after several days.

Tamara, a project manager from the Balkans, justified hiring a housekeeper when it became clear to her that it would save her family money. She calculated that paying someone to buy and prep food from the local markets at local prices was cheaper than buying ready-to-eat provisions at the European-style supermarkets. To illustrate for me, she did the calculation from memory about how much each jar of Barilla pasta sauce would cost versus buying bulk tomatoes, onions, and garlic at the local price at an outdoor market. The cheap cost of the housekeeper's labor didn't make up the difference—and that was without even factoring in the monetary value of Tamara's time as a skilled laborer who could be working at her office job instead of processing tomatoes into sauce.

Alain, an employee of a French NGO focused on drought and famine, knew he and his girlfriend needed a housekeeper to cook and clean because of their long work hours. "If we wanted fresh food, and if we didn't want to eat kebab or take-out for the ninth night in a row, and if you come back at nine in the evening from work . . ." Alain had tried to do his own housework in previous African posts, to disastrous results, including attempting to do his own laundry by hand. "I was never very good at it," he admitted. "I never got the soap flakes out."

It was especially European and American aid workers who felt this initial discomfort with having help in their home. Alma, the country director of a faith-based NGO who grew up in Latin America, didn't feel the same awkwardness as her US counterparts. "I'm from a developing country," she explained, "and having house helpers is normal. It's not a new thing to me and I don't have any mixed feelings about that. Seriously. As long as, to me, as long as we pay a salary that is fair and cover, you know, the healthcare and everything, that's another job." For those who came from poorer countries, the very visible hierarchies of wealth that entitled professional people to hire poorer people to clean their homes were not something to be ashamed of or uncomfortable about, but merely a reality.

Alain said his non-Western colleagues were the ones who broke him of his idea of trying to not have domestic help. "I was talking to a friend of mine who grew up in Mumbai. She was like, 'I never sort of understood the Western abhorrence of it, because you're not doing anything by avoiding it. Doing your own laundry does nothing to reverse colonial power relations.'" As he grew to see it, insisting on doing his own domestic work was "performative." "I think after a few years you get rid of the performative aspects, and the most important part is just not being a dick. That's really the most important part. And just realizing that you're an employer. And kind of being the employer that you wish you had."

THE OBLIGATION

Doing your own laundry may do nothing to reverse colonial power relations, as Alain put it, but for some it is even more insidious. Two different Canadians in Dakar told me with apparent derision that a certain high-level Canadian diplomat and his wife didn't hire a housekeeper in Dakar because the wife insisted on doing the housework herself. The gossip-worthy elements of this rumor were twofold: one, it suggested a retrograde wife's-place-is-in-the-home kind of gender politics that my two interlocutors found shameful and embarrassing, and two, it was a selfish act. With a salary like his, the diplomat should be creating a job opportunity for one (or several) local people to wash his floors, rather than having his wife do this reproductive labor for free.

Many aid workers framed their employment of domestic workers as an act of duty or obligation. As Jillian, the regional director for a faith-based INGO said, "It's kind of like this mixed thing. You feel like especially in American culture, you know, I can do it all myself. We're independent. We don't have people clean for us. But at the same time, it's also this, 'Okay, it actually is a good opportunity.' And that's where you do feel good about it. You're like, 'Okay, I make a pretty good living and . . .' So it's kind of this mixed thing." Rather than sitting in the feelings of discomfort at outsourcing aspects of life maintenance that could ostensibly be done by oneself, Jillian and others reframed their role as one of job creators and thus could "feel good about it."

Even before she made her financial calculations about tomato sauce, Tamara and her husband felt pressured to take on a house cleaner at their first African post, in East Africa. "We had no intention of hiring anyone local or anything. My husband and I are so self-sufficient, we felt like that was a waste of money. But then our guard of our building was like, two weeks into our stay, 'If you need somebody to clean, my wife, she's a cleaner. She used to clean the apartment that you guys are living in.' And we were like, 'No thanks.' And then he kinda . . . it came up two or three times." Tamara framed her decision to finally hire the guard's wife not because she—the primary breadwinner for the family—had a second child but glossed over that change in her need for hired care and pointed to their sense of obligation. "And then I had another baby, yeah. But I mean at the time, and I remember having this conversation, like, 'I feel like he feels like we need to do this because this was his wife's livelihood and income.' So I remember the moment when I realized, like, we owed it to this person; it was part of our role as an expat to hire someone local. We had this obligation, like he kind of made it known that, you know, his wife was without an income because the family that had lived there moved. And if I chose not to hire her, she would continue to not have an income. And he had three kids to feed. So I was like, 'Okay.'"

Turning the purchase of cheap domestic labor into a kind of noblesse oblige is a deft way to displace guilt and discomfort about privilege and the outsourcing of highly gendered reproductive labor. This kind of pivot can be seen more broadly in the development industry, as self-serving acts of career advancement or life enhancement are presented as acts of altruism or care for the poor.[5] Indeed, the narrative of an obligation to intervene for the good of the other is part of the depoliticization of poverty that characterizes the international development industry.[6] It goes without saying that the philosophy of the burden to help the less fortunate was also used as a justification for all sorts of colonial interventions as well.[7]

Gwyneth was coming around to the idea of having someone come twice a week to clean her apartment. "I should make the most of some of those perks of living somewhere like here, where it's entirely acceptable, normal, affordable and it's a nice thing to be putting money back into all these people. And actually, we have a cleaning lady at the office that wants extra hours, so I'm like . . ." Gwyneth was still reckoning with the fact that this was not act of posh excess but rather an "entirely acceptable, normal" thing to do. The most convincing argument for her, however, was that she knew it would be good for the cleaning lady to have another gig. It was "a nice thing" to do, in fact. This opportunity to do something helpful for someone less fortunate was the most effective reframing she needed to talk herself into paying someone meager wages to clean her home.

A GOOD BOSS

As I've noted in earlier chapters, domestic workers and aid workers generally agree that the pay and the work conditions are much better in expat households than in Senegalese homes. Aid workers not only eagerly promote their fairness and flexibility as a group, but individual aid workers also tout their qualities in relation to fellow expats. Rayna, for example, saw herself as a good boss in distinction to other expats. "I don't think other people treat their help as nicely as we do," she told me after outlining the responsibilities of her nanny and housekeeper. "People are very demanding, and they don't pay, and they come home late. And for me, I feel guilty. Like I make sure I call and be like, 'Is it okay I'm running late?' I'm always conscious of their lives as well, and I don't think some others are." She described herself explicitly as "a good boss," explaining further that "a good boss treats their employees well. And treats them fair. And I think people take advantage of the household help."

Rayna noted that there were benefits to being a good boss. "I find that because I treat them well, they don't mind staying a little bit late and helping with little things." Her nanny had recently agreed to shift her schedule, taking on a weekend or two each month without additional pay because her weekly hours had been reduced when the youngest child started school full time. Lan (2003, 526) draws on Nakano Glenn (1986) to note that employers deploy what has been called "strategic personalism" with their house help, meaning that they use kindness and intimacy in particular ways to ensure the quality of care work that they desire.[8]

In other contexts, researchers have shown that employers of domestic workers deploy personalism as a way to "reduce class boundaries and alleviate [their] class guilt" (Alvarez Tinajero 2014). Having friendly relations minimizes the social separation and allows the employer to imagine that the employee is an equal and not in a position of subordination. This can mean anything from sharing personal information to calling each other by first names in an effort to keep an appearance of informality in the relationship, as though the employer and employee are co-workers and not engaged in a hierarchical relationship of power.

In the case of expat aid workers in Senegal, personalism can also be an effort to minimize racial guilt. American employers felt particular discomfort with the optics of employing black domestic employees due to their country's long history linking racial oppression and domestic labor, from slavery through the Jim Crow era and to the present. Meredith, describing her feelings of unease in employing domestic help in West Africa and how they differed from her experiences in aid work in the Middle East, said, "I'm American, you know how it is. We have this history between whites and blacks and that does color the way you look at Africa."

Carly recounted how her understanding of the history of race relations in America shaped her relations with her first maid in Senegal. "It was so funny because when we moved here it was right after that movie *The Help* came out and it was so fresh in my mind, and it was one of those things that you just have to get used to. It just doesn't seem right." *The Help*, an Oscar-winning Hollywood adaptation of a novel by a white author about black domestic workers in the US South, has been criticized for its softening and trivializing of segregation.[9] By suddenly being in a position to hire a black woman to do her cleaning now that she was in Senegal, Carly felt transported back in time to the Jim Crow era and it didn't "seem right."

One of the dodgy messages of *The Help* and other movies that whitewash America's violent history of racism is that there were mean, racist bosses of black domestics during Jim Crow but also "good bosses" like the book and film's protagonist, a white woman. Carly was determined to be the latter. Recalling a central plot point from the movie, in which black maids were not allowed to use the same toilets as the families they worked for, she told of an incident in her first weeks of employing her maid in her home. "She had, like, upstairs on the roof there was like a squatty potty[10] and a little spigot shower, and I was like, 'You know, you can use our bathroom!' Because this thing from *The Help* was in my mind about having separate bathrooms, right? For the help. And I was like, 'Oh no, that's not going to happen here!'" Carly laughed at her earlier panic that she would turn out to be one of the bad bosses.

Despite her desire to uphold her own self-image as a non-racist, good boss, she eventually had to reframe her understanding of the bathroom situation to accommodate her employee's wishes. She continued, "But what I didn't realize was that it's actually considered an honor for them to have their own bathroom and their own space. They want that. That makes them feel appreciated. And so, for me, that was a big . . . I had to shift how I viewed that. She kept using the upstairs. And even now, our house helper, Agnès, will not use any of our bathrooms. Like she has her own little space and she uses that. But yeah, that took some getting used to." Carly was surprised to learn that her maid would want to have a separate bathroom where she could have privacy from the family. Pleased and comforted to think that this was "an honor" for her housekeepers, she could relinquish her desire to control where her employee used the bathroom and reframe this separation in this gratifying way rather than as an underlining of the maid's subservience.[11]

Several aid workers told me negative stories that their domestic workers had clearly relayed to them about previous employers. These included details about boundary keeping—such as insisting on being called "Monsieur" or "Madame" instead of their first name or not allowing the help to use the cutlery—that clearly scandalized the aid workers relating them, with their connotations of openly racist ideas of impurity.[12] Others judged fellow expats for being too demanding of their workers more generally, and as Rayna put it, not being "conscious of their lives."

Sylvie, a French employee of an organization that focuses on maternal and child health, compared herself favorably with her nanny's former employer, who she dubbed "très maniaque," or obsessive compulsive. She found that her nanny was conditioned to be precise about all the details. "And I am far from being someone, really *far* from being someone who looks at that. Sometimes I have to tell [the nanny], 'Relax, relax!'" She surmised that her nanny's previous employer must have being extremely strict and domineering, and Sylvie was eager to tell me how much more easygoing she was as a boss. As an example of her low-maintenance attitude toward housekeeping, Sylvie said that the bedroom didn't have to be cleaned every single day. "The kitchen, the bathrooms, yes, but for the rest . . ."

Gemma similarly portrayed herself as a laid-back employer. "It's just that I am very hands off and lazy about managing my household staff and so I just, you know, let her do what she does." Being a laid-back boss was an important quality of a good boss, because it intimated that the employer did not feel entitled to this domestic labor. To be precise and demanding would indicate a sense of imperious entitlement ill-fitting a self-image that claims to, in the words of the Stuff EAWs Like post, "see all humanity as their brethren, nobody inherently more noble or deserving than the next."

Gemma did think about firing her maid, not because of her cleaning but because the maid seemed uncomfortable around Gemma. It drove Gemma crazy that her maid avoided her and would barely speak to her at first. Her husband insisted the maid was simply shy, but Gemma felt her aloofness as a personal affront, citing particularly that her maid would slip in and out of the house without finding Gemma and greeting her. "She actually kind of really annoyed me, and she doesn't really chat with me. Not that I need someone to chat with me but I'd like to actually have somewhat of a rapport when you're in my house all the time." A lack of rapport made Gemma more aware of the social distance between herself and her employee, ruining the illusion of friendly equality that a more sociable relationship could help her maintain.

For similar reasons, Carly ultimately chose not hire a maid who came to clean for a trial period. Although the woman was a good cleaner, she "didn't say a word the entire time that she was there." Carly explained, "She was not friendly, you know . . . not . . . didn't have any interactions with us." The woman Carly did eventually hire was not a particularly good cleaner. "Like we'll go through and there'll just be, like, part of a cabinet that she hasn't dusted at all. Or instead of picking up pictures and dusting under them, she'll just dust around them and you just have this pile of dust." Carly laughed as she said this. "And honestly I don't really care about that kind of thing. It was more important having somebody in the house that I enjoyed being around, that didn't feel awkward, that the kids liked. The kids love her." Having an awkward relationship with the house help highlighted the breach of intimacy in having a non-family member in your home.

Aid workers wanted their employees to walk a particular line of being comfortable but not too comfortable in their homes. Two told stories of other expats' maids who had been fired for too much familiarity and comfort. One aid worker colleague of Alice's returned home to find his housekeeper hosting a guest in his home. "That's kind of a violation," Alice commented. Another aid worker told of a colleague who saw on her maid's Facebook page that the maid was wearing her hat and taking selfies. "It was not like this was a hat that was just laying out," my interlocutor said with an air of scandal. "It was something put away." These two cases display what my aid worker interlocutors (as well as their expat friends who are the subjects of the anecdotes in question) saw as clear violations of the boundaries that domestic workers should respect. These unspoken boundaries are meant to protect against "the threat of mixing" (Ozyegin 2001, 11) that is ever present in intimate labor. In both cases, the maid was fired.

A MEMBER OF THE FAMILY

Like most aid workers I spoke to, for Amanda, an American in her early thirties who worked for an international NGO in nutrition and food security, the basics of the boundaries between herself and her employees were not intuitive. "For me it was a hard transition into being an employer," she remarked. When I asked her to elaborate, she said, "It's just, like, the responsibility of hiring someone and then the fear a little bit of—I've heard in different places, like, it can be exciting or it can be a little nerve-wracking that they become part of your family. And I was really intimidated by that. And I think once you, like, cross those boundaries, everyone always says it's easier and I kind of know it will be, rationally, but, I don't know, you don't always think rationally about those things." Amanda found the prospect of intimacy with intimate laborers daunting and was uncertain how to manage that.

Other aid workers told stories of the dangers of getting too intimate with domestic workers. One danger in their itinerant profession was simply getting too emotionally attached to house staff and then feeling the rupture of the relationship at the inevitable end of the tour. This was particularly common with nannies, as their role as caretakers of children led most naturally to emotional attachment. Alma spoke of the heartbreak she felt in saying goodbye to a nanny at a previous post. "The day we left, we were bawling, and my son was so confused. The two women he loved the most were, like, so sad." The event left a mark on her, "because it affected me for many, many years. I couldn't talk about her without still, like, crying." Alma realized she couldn't get so attached to her house help. Care, she discovered, could feel good, but it could also be a burden and a source of pain. "So after that, my relationship with the nannies has been more distant. You want them to be family while they're working with you . . ." Alma trailed off, finding it difficult to put into words the very particular kind of bounded intimacy (see chapter 2) that she and other expat aid workers desired from their intimate employees.

Much of the feminist literature on the feelings of care work explores these fraught issues of being close but not too close. Whereas the condescension of care for the poor in development is usually framed as "paternalism," the condescension of care for domestic servants is cast as "maternalism." This reflects both the highly gendered nature of domestic work itself and of this sphere of labor in which employees and employers are usually female. In this context, in which the employers are also aid workers, there is a mix of both paternalistic ideas of development and maternalistic approaches to treating house staff.

Maternalism is characterized by an obfuscation of the economic relationship between domestic workers and their employers by portraying it as a familial relationship. Employees are treated like "members of the family" selectively in ways that are usually controlled by the employer.[13] Some expat aid workers I interviewed described their employees in this way; nannies, maids, guards, and even gardeners were sometimes described as "part of the family." The ads I surveyed in chapter 1 sometimes used this terminology as well. Being a member of the family could mean a broad range of things to individual aid workers, from simply getting along well with the family to being beloved by the children, to being forgiven for breaking dishes, to, as I describe below, being taken under the employer's wing like a little sibling or a son or daughter.

Scholars of domestic workers are clear that even well-intentioned maternalism is a site of uneven power relations and can "heighten the structural asymmetries of the employment relationship" (Alvarez Tinajero 2014, 68).[14] As Anderson notes, "For the employer there are clear advantages to the obfuscation of the employment relationship, since it seriously weakens the employee's negotiating position in terms of wages and conditions—any attempt to improve these are an insult to the 'family'" (2000, 123). Being part of the family in a conditional and contingent manner can make domestic workers more vulnerable rather than less vulnerable.

Keith, who works for the UN, spoke with evident distress about a nanny named Thérèse who had stopped coming to work after his family returned from a holiday in his native US. "She disappeared—not disappeared like in an airplane crash or something, we just didn't see her." Keith was particularly disturbed by the abrupt rupture with the nanny on behalf of his children. "It's really weird. Because she would have had—first of all, you're working with a family for three years. You're watching these beautiful kids grow up. How do you leave these kids and then not say goodbye or say anything?" Though he said the children were not very upset by the change—"they don't know what's normal or what's not normal"—Keith himself was still mentally going through his past interactions with the nanny to look for clues as to her indifference to his children. "If she could just go and leave the kids like that, I don't know, I think . . . I'd go to the breakfast table, where she'd be sitting with the kids and she'd have earphones in her ears while the kids were eating breakfast. It's like, Thérèse, you can do that when the kids go to school, but right now . . ."

Later in our conversation, it came up that Keith and his wife had been contemplating firing Thérèse before they departed for the trip during which she left them. Another household employee had accused Thérèse of snooping in Keith's wife's phone, and although they weren't sure they could trust the accuser, Keith's wife was eager to terminate her employment after this alleged breach of privacy. Keith's understanding of what Thérèse's attachment to his children should be after watching the beautiful kids grow up for three years was that it should be strong enough to prevent her from leaving without saying goodbye to them, but not strong enough to prevent him and his wife from removing her from the household because of a suspected indiscretion. The obfuscation of the employment relationship is entirely contingent: when employers wish to assert the lack of familial obligation they have with these non-familial household members, they have the power and authority to do so.

A NICE BOSS

This is not to say that firing staff was easy for all expat aid workers in Dakar. For some employers, their eagerness to be seen as a nice boss led to some absurd outcomes. Kim told me scornfully of her American neighbors who were so conflict-averse that they went to great lengths to adapt to a bad situation rather than fire their housekeeper. "We had people in my building—the housekeeper (they didn't have any kids) stole! Money! And she's still working. They were like, 'Well, we got a safe and so now we put the money in the safe.'" She laughed in disbelief, "I'm like, 'Are you kidding?' They're like, 'Well, we're not here much longer, and we feel bad because she has three kids . . . She supports a whole family.' And I'm like, 'Dude! You can't have somebody steal!' But it's something that you have to learn," she concluded, about the art of firing someone. "I had to learn it."

Termination of employment is another site that brings the real power structure between employer and employee into relief

(Hondagneu-Sotelo 2007). You do not "fire" members of the family. A laid-back, nice boss who is not exacting and feels equal to all of humanity does not take away the livelihood of a much poorer person with dependent relations. To avoid confronting not only the employee but the reality of unequal power relations, expat aid workers like Kim's neighbor and Jessica, below, simply tried to endure and outwait a bad domestic situation.

Jessica did not like her first housekeeper in Dakar, but it took her two years to fire her. "I didn't want to really mess with her. I didn't want to deal with it." Jessica, whose job involves dropping into conflict zones and confronting violence in high stakes scenarios, did not want to face the unpleasantness of dismissing a household employee. Jessica spent two years disliking and resenting her housekeeper and then finally sidestepped the issue by moving to a new home in Dakar. "We moved houses, so I felt like that was my clean break, I would get someone new." Even then, Jessica was unwilling to let her housekeeper know how unhappy she had been with her work, so she made up a story about it not being convenient to have her maid in the new home, gave her three months of severance pay, and then quietly hired another maid once she moved.

The US Foreign Service handbook has recommendations for American expats about firing house staff overseas that similarly emphasize the need to avoid making a scene:

> If you need to dismiss employees, do not give them advance warning. Simply ask for the keys, give them the required severance pay, and ask them to leave. Try to avoid firing someone in a moment of anger. Take the time to find out in advance what local regulations are and the best way to handle the situation in the context of the local culture. "Saving face" may be important in some cultures; in other countries you may need a signed statement from the employee saying that he or she has been paid in full. Regardless of the reason, try to avoid firing someone before a major holiday. (Foreign Service Institute 2016, 222)

I heard other stories of aid workers going to great lengths to avoid conflict with their domestic employees and bending over backward to display their qualities as a nice boss. Alice was not happy with her maid Diariatou's cleaning. She admitted to being "kind of OCD" about cleaning. "Yeah. It's not . . . it's not perfect," She laughed. "But it's okay." When I asked Alice if she could talk to Diariatou and show her what she did or didn't like, she demurred. "I could, I could. But we don't really overlap that much because she comes when I'm at work. And . . . it's fine. It's fine. This is Senegal. Things are going to get dusty. You know." Alice would rather deal with her home being not as clean as she preferred than confront Diariatou with her dissatisfaction.

Alice was very concerned about having a good relationship with Diariatou and spoke haltingly, with evident unease, about their dynamic. "I think we have a good relationship. I think she would . . . I think she's really happy to work with us. She just seems very . . . she just seems very easy . . . she's just so . . . You know, there are . . . Senegalese people are usually . . . don't really have problems, you know? If you don't have an issue with them, they usually don't have an issue with you. But at the same time, you don't really know if they would actually confront you with an issue if they had one!" Multiple times in our discussions, Alice expressed doubt and worry about whether Diariatou was happy working for her. When telling me the salary she paid Diariatou, about $130 a month to come three mornings a week, she added quickly that the salary "isn't huge. I would maybe even pay her a little more. I always feel bad. I know that she's got, like, three kids. I live in Dakar; it's expensive."

For her part, Diariatou was mostly satisfied with her hours and her pay and found her bosses to be good people, if a bit baffling in their over-the-top efforts to be undemanding. In my interview with her, she recounted several instances of confusion that arose from their avoiding asking her directly for what they wanted. Alice, she described as having "a pure heart," and her husband, Marco, as "even crazier than his wife" in all his kindness and superciliousness. To illustrate and underline how kind they were, she told me a long story about how she had wanted to travel home to the Casamance in the south of Senegal to visit her father for the first time in five years. She had hoped to take advantage of a US holiday, which would normally have meant a long weekend for her, to make the long trip, but when she informed Alice and Marco of her plans, they were distraught. Alice's relatives were coming to Senegal for a visit at that same time and they were counting on Diariatou to stay and take care of the cat while the couple took their family for a vacation to a seaside town a few hours south of Dakar.

For Diariatou, this was not a big problem, and she quickly said she'd go see her father another time. "I didn't want to, you know . . . I didn't want to ruin their thing. You understand? The aunt came from far away. I have the duty to stay and watch the house." She remembers that Alice continued to insist that Diariatou go on her scheduled trip home. Diariatou recalls that Alice was "desperate." "She said, 'No, no, no. That's just not right.'" Alice's deep discomfort with her power over Diariatou as an employer made her frantic and frustrated. Diariatou remembers Alice and Marco arguing in English about it in front of her and Alice being near tears. "I was just watching, I don't understand a word," Diaratou recalled, baffled. "Really, they are nice people."

Diariatou did cancel her trip, and Alice and her family took their vacation, but Alice continued to feel lousy about what had transpired, and Diariatou had to spend time and energy making Alice feel better about something that had worked out in Alice's favor. In a conversation with me, not knowing that Diariatou had related the same incident to me in my interview with her, Alice brought up the canceled trip to the Casamance with evident guilt and frustration. "I feel so bad," she wailed. "She'll probably never ask for a vacation again!" Alice's concern for her treatment of her employee did not ultimately result in a better situation for Diariatou. Though Diariatou did think her bosses were nice, she was not materially better off than if they had been demanding or direct. An outsized concern about being nice and being liked is a way to work out feelings of discomfort and guilt about larger, structural issues of inequity and privilege that being nice does little to redress.[15]

IMPROVING LIVES

As a matter of course, the majority of aid workers I interviewed told me about some kind of "help" they offered to their domestic staff outside the fee-for-services employment relationship. When I asked if the domestic worker had children, I routinely got an answer similar to that of Alain: "She does, so we help out. One of her kids is in France, so we pay for his tuition." From paying school fees for children to paying for literacy classes for adults, cooking classes, and training of various kinds, many aid workers were engaged in a project of improving the lives of their workers. They vastly preferred this kind of engagement—giving money for a specific project—to direct handouts. Expat aid workers routinely positioned themselves not just as the *patron* (French for boss) of their domestic workers, but as patron as well, contributing beneficently and on their own terms to the causes in the lives of their workers that spoke to them.

Fiona, who was preparing to leave Dakar when I met her, was contemplating what role she would play in the life of her house staff when she returned to Europe. Throughout her time in Dakar, she had taken seriously the responsibility she felt she and her husband had as *patrons*, giving life and financial advice to her staff as well as running a tight ship in the home. She had played a guiding role in her nanny Florence's life in particular, providing advice and counsel, as well as loans or monetary gifts toward certain expenses that Fiona believed were good investments. Fiona disapproved of Florence and her husband's choice to use their savings to buy a piece of land outside Dakar, where they could afford it. Fiona described this land as "out in the middle of nowhere" and thought it was an impractical choice given that there was no possibility of finding domestic work with expats in its peri-urban location. She opted against contributing to the purchase, telling me, "I could have, we could have . . ." but that she and her husband did not help with the project because they thought it was so ill-considered.

They did, however, want to continue to invest in Florence's gifted daughter, whom she described as "really bright. Like *really* bright." Fiona expressed appreciative approval of Florence's commitment to finding the best schools for her children. "Education is the big thing. Because she sees our education, you know." Fiona believed she and her husband had inspired Florence with how education had shaped their own lives and she felt education was the best avenue for investing resources in Florence after they left. "I'm like, 'Okay, so how can we help that?' I was telling [my husband], 'Is there a portion we can fund for a period of time or a number of years, that can be our kind of connection with those people?' Or not! We don't know. I haven't decided."

She did want to keep connected with the house staff and her idea was to continue her role as donor in their lives, with "some type of peppered support system over time." She noted, "I work for [a large, faith-based development agency], you know. We have child sponsorship programs; we have all sorts all over the world . . . So if it were within our means, then that's something I would consider." Fiona framed her desire to support Florence's effort to advance her daughter's education as a parallel to her development agency's famous child sponsorship program.[16] She put herself in the role of developer and her nanny in the role of target population or beneficiary. This was a distortion or at least a very partial perception of what their relationship was based on, which was an employment relationship where Florence provided salaried caring labor for Fiona's family. That Fiona saw her role in Florence's life as benefactor and advisor gave Fiona the opportunity to feel even more power and esteem from her relationship with Florence, in addition to extracting her reproductive labor.

Like Fiona, who took her development agency as a model for how to engage with her house staff, Tamara used programming from her agency in relating to her first household employee. Tamara's housekeeper had been asking for loans, including just days after being paid her salary. For Tamara this suggested not that the salary was far too low to cover her housekeeper's living expenses but that she needed Tamara to teach her how to manage money. "I said, 'You need some financial service training!' So I sat with her and said, 'What are your bills? When are they due? When you get paid at the start of the month, maybe no one ever told you, you need to plan for your water bill, your electricity bill. Pay that first! Set aside the rest.'" Tamara laughed, saying, "I was bringing some of our programming work that we do in the village to, like, help her." Tamara described this effort to educate her employee as "empowering" her housekeeper.

Nancy, an American in her early fifties who worked in sustainable agriculture, paid her house staff according to her own philosophy of responsible giving. For example, when disclosing what she paid her housekeeper, of whom she said, "I sort of see her like my daughter," she explained, "What I do is I don't pay a really high salary. I pay 80,000—it's a small apartment—but then I give her money for other things." Roughly $130 a month for five full days a week was certainly below the rate that most expats paid their staff regardless of the size of the apartment, but Nancy preferred to give a low monthly salary and then to say yes to various requests from her housekeeper that she felt were worthy, including covering medical bills for her daughter or paying for English language lessons and night school. Nancy was hesitant in explaining her reasons for this choice to me. "I hate to say this—it sounds so un-PC—but when the Senegalese staff that I've had has a good sum of money, the majority of them are not responsible and don't know how to save money. And can't save it." She recounted a story of her previous security guard, Abdou. She had given Abdou a substantial raise when she increased his duties to watering the garden and walking the dogs, and shortly thereafter, he disappeared. She found out that he had taken this new influx of cash and used it to migrate to southern Africa, leaving Nancy without a guard. "After that, I realized that giving big lump sums of money to somebody doesn't create the most responsible behavior."

Nancy backtracked a bit from this statement, giving instead a cultural argument rather than an individual one for employees' behavior. "I shouldn't say 'irresponsible.' I'm putting a judgment on it. The whole concept of being able to save money, when you have someone in your family that is needy, that really needs something, you know, you're required to help. And you just can't save it—it's considered irresponsible if you do that. Another cultural aspect. So they're unable to save money because there is always somebody in the family that's going to need money." For Nancy, it was the Senegalese population at large that could not be counted on to be responsible with their money. This attitude mirrors the way that aid dollars are often given not directly to governments—which are assumed to be full of corruption and self-interest—but funneled through NGOs, which are presumed to have only technocratic ideals and goals.[17] Nancy's idea of how money should be used correctly—to be saved, not invested in family or personal networks or in migration—is here framed not as culturally American but as responsible.

When aid workers feel that they are acting as developers, as donors, as beneficent guides for their domestic staff, improving their lives and investing in their future well-being, they are able to ignore or dilute some of the potentially troubling aspects of their position. Taking advantage of their relative wealth and privilege to outsource the low-status work in their home and paying rates far below what they themselves would accept as a living wage in their own country does not fit with their perceptions of their purpose as an aid worker in Africa. Enjoying the fruits of the power and wealth disparities between their home nation and their host nation is potentially disturbing and distressing to the aid worker and must be reframed so as to keep consistent their self-image of being on the right side of global justice.[18]

Reframing the outside gifts or guidance as charitable or even as a form of aid work allows aid workers to disavow "the morally suspect or commercial in nature" (Wo 2019, 165) aspects of their relationships with domestic workers and preserve what the Stuff EAWs Like blog post refers to as their "delicate psychological equilibrium." They are not simply paying someone to clean their bathrooms and drive their children around. They are providing a livelihood, contributing to a family, building the capacities of those who they thereby consider under their care as much as the other way around. Monetary gifts and paying medical bills get rebranded not as supplementing what is a very low wage for hard work in an expensive city but as gestures of charity and generosity.

As aid workers elide this "different facet of moral labor" (Fechter 2016) in the home with their work in development, it makes sense that the underlying maternalist and paternalist impulses of both overlap. Sabrina Hom (2007) notes that maternalism in a domestic work relationship can be infantilizing: "Maternalistic employers believe they are rescuing their unfortunate employees from poverty and ignorance; they care for their 'childlike' employees with love, guidance, and gifts as much as or more than with wages and benefits. Maternalism obscures workers' position as economic agents and independent adults, casting them instead as dependent children" (28). The development industry's paternalism has long been similarly accused of casting the poor, especially Africans, as helpless children who cannot handle their own affairs.[19]

I find Bornstein's insight into what she calls "impulsive philanthropy" helpful: "Impulsive philanthropy does not offer rights to recipients; it offers help and sustenance according to the will of the donor. For donors, gifts may provide merit, meaning and in some cases even a transformative experience" (2012, 172). But to the recipients, the rewards may be less meaningful and much less transformational. Gift-giving in the category of maternalism, like other forms of maternalism, serves to reinforce the subordination of the employee and "pre-empt or avert employees' demands" (172).

Expat aid workers have ambivalent feelings about their domestic staff. They feel obligated; they feel guilty. Having domestic help is awkward and frustrating and luxurious and essential all at once. They resent their help as much as they feel grateful and dependent on them. It is never perfect; it is always more than you deserve and not the way you want it. Their feelings of class and racial guilt are challenged by their feelings of vulnerability as described in chapter 2. Two contradictory profiles emerge of their house staff: "deceitful but also victims in need of saving and financial assistance" (Wo 2019, 165). We have so much, they have so little. Where is my change? Is he too lazy? Is she secretly wearing my hat when I'm not home? Various strategies are employed to reframe and deflect and absolve the discomfort that comes with hiring intimate laborers whose lives can be improved with the meagerest of wages to do tasks you would normally do yourself for free.

Many aid workers I spoke to were self-reflexive not only about their relations with their domestic staff but about their role in Senegal and in the development industry more generally. The vast majority entered the industry with a sincere desire to dedicate their effort and energy to make the world more equitable. After years in the development industry, however, they had a more modest understanding about their potential to make an impact on the persistent structures of inequity that shape the possibilities for sustainable change. The global status quo was stubborn and reinforced at every turn. Poor countries weren't *really* going to pull themselves out of poverty. They felt the disconnect between their daily paper-pushing of the boulder up the hill and the acute and seemingly cemented need all around them.

Just as doing one's own laundry does nothing to reverse colonial power relations, pushing back at the development industry's framing and limitations is unlikely to right a very large ship that is carried by the currents of neoliberal capital and a long history of global white supremacy. Besides, the laundry needs doing. Not taking a larger salary than local hires, not living in comfortable housing paid for by dollars earmarked for poverty reduction, not taking advantage of the market rates for care work wouldn't change the global power geometry. Would it?

CONCLUSION

IN THIS BOOK, I HAVE taken a closer look at a commonplace yet overlooked relationship in development—namely, between expat aid workers and their domestic staff. I have argued that these relationships put a spotlight on the extractive aspects of the development industry, how Western professionals mine not only financial and career advancement opportunities from this industry, reaping great rewards from development dollars targeted at lifting poor communities out of poverty, but also reproductive labor from local people that is instrumental not only in performing their work but in fashioning and reproducing their class status. Though not the ostensible "beneficiaries" of development, Western aid workers can gain a great deal of sustainable, transformative value through their participation in the industry. Take the example of Gemma, who not only moved up her career ladder through posts overseas but was able to pay off student loans and a mortgage, send her children to exclusive top schools, and spend more time and energy with her spouse and children while also caring for herself.

The domestic workers that aid workers employ, on the other hand, though not seen as "practitioners" of the development industry, are nevertheless instrumental to reproducing the labor of their employers, as they tend to their children and their homes. In return they receive wages and work conditions that, while superior to the local domestic service labor market, do not provide for sustainable upward mobility. Many are compelled to separate from their children and spouses to migrate to the city to find employment. Working for a rotating, transient group of expats makes them susceptible to periods of unemployment and ruptures in their earning. The informal, word-of-mouth methods of hiring and the climate of perceived insecurity among aid workers makes them vulnerable to whims and goodwill of their employers. Madeleine's case is illustrative—after over twenty years of working in expat homes, she had little savings, little control over her next employment opportunity, and didn't feel empowered to ask her employer for the wages and work conditions she desired. Domestic labor is grueling physical work, and as Madeleine neared retirement age, she had no clear path to financial security or retirement.

On the face of it, Gemma and Madeleine have many things in common. Both are mothers; both are responsible for the double day; both want to support their families with their wage-earning labor. Neither woman is citizen of a state that provides for the needs of family care; in both the US and in Senegal, caring labor is privatized and families must make arrangements for themselves. This is the case across the globe, and a necessary larger reckoning with work culture and gendered domestic labor has yet to happen. Aging populations in many countries and a reduction in the number of multigenerational households have intensified the need and demand for caregiving services. Welfare regimes also shape the organization of care within and across countries and societies: as fewer public care options are accessible, care needs are increasingly met through in-home caregiving services. Instead of a widespread societal confronting of the changing needs of families, informal and un-overseen labor arrangements are made by hiring caretakers, generally other women, to do the work for low pay.

This privatization has very different consequences for women separated by class and by nation. Class and citizenship and race intervene to impede solidarity.[1] Indeed, the burdens of privatization "lead to the formation of direct relations of inequality between them" as "women from richer countries transfer their burdens of the double day to women from poorer countries" (Parreñas 2008, 172). In the context of expat aid workers and local Senegalese domestic workers, as in most iterations of the social organization of care globally and historically, the rights of those who command others to care are racialized and gendered and based on a coercion of restricted choice (Glenn 2012, 5–7).

The development literature treats the question of "gender" in a narrow way. Women are increasingly the "targets" of development, as agencies like Gemma's have in recent years put their focus on gender inequalities through "gender and development" or "women in development" programming.[2] These movements respond to the fact that women had long been ignored in development initiatives. As is to be expected with neoliberal approaches to development, most of their efforts champion empowering women primarily because they are believed to be an efficient means to lift families and communities out of poverty.[3] This book reveals another facet of gender engaged through the development industry: namely, how the international circulation of Western development professionals produces a class of gendered care workers to do their domestic labor.

Though other forms of Western migration to Africa, including mining or private industry, produce and exploit the same labor pool, there is no inherent paradox between their industries' raisons d'être and their impact. Aid workers like Gemma have devoted their careers to an industry whose stated aim is to improve well-being and increase prosperity around the globe. How can they reconcile this mission with the personal perks and wealth extraction they collect from the industry? How can they be at ease when their salaries are so far superior to those around them, when the opportunity to wash their dishes and empty their garbage appears advantageous to many? As I've shown, aid workers are uncomfortable with the inequity they inhabit in the field and they develop strategies to mitigate it, including withdrawing into securitized bubbles, treating domestic staff like burdens—as if managing staff is one of the "hardship" aspects of their overseas post—and framing their own domestic employees as mini development projects. Though the wages they pay are below the standards of their home countries, which already value care work quite low, their favorable comparison with the local market can assuage feelings of guilt about exploitation.

Researchers of the global care chain acknowledge that the practical and ethical issues at the intersection of care and power cannot be solved by individuals and individual families making different choices, but through policy change that addresses the "care deficit" through a provision of social services. Similarly, I am not arguing here that individual aid workers must be seen as at fault for engaging workers for hire for domestic labor. Rather, aid organizations themselves could begin to reckon with and regulate these informal work relationships. One way to begin this work would be an examination of the structures within the development industry that make these arrangements so common, including the widespread practice of expat hiring.

Do expatriate aid workers need to be in the field at all? Do they need to take the perks and inflated "hardship pay" salaries out of already overextended programming budgets? Could local workers fill these posts and do the same work without these expenses? These questions come up repeatedly in calls for localization in aid work. *Localization* is defined as a process in which "international humanitarian actors shift power and responsibilities of development and humanitarian aid efforts toward local and national actors" (Blum 2020). This is not merely a process of hiring more local people but involves working toward local control of project conceptualization and management (Bonacker, von Heusinger, and Zimmer 2019), as well as examining power structures that lead to local NGOs wielding so little power (Michael 2004). Numerous studies have shown that the model of expatriate employment in aid work brings with it specific problems, like "chronic mobility" (Nowicka 2006) and a high rate of turnover that "has implications for organizational memory, project continuity and the development of local expertise" (Loquercio, Hammersley, and Emmens 2006), not to mention an "inclination to 'reinvent the wheel'" (Hunt 2011, 609) and a detrimental impact on relationships with local actors.[4]

The COVID-19 pandemic has brought renewed attention to the idea of localization. In the early days of lockdowns and travel restrictions, expatriate aid workers all over the world scrambled to figure out whether to fly home from their overseas posts, in many cases straight into the epicenter of the pandemic, or risk being stuck far from family and in places with few resources to handle an outbreak. Many were being barred from returning to the field from their vacations or trips to HQ because of unprecedented restrictions on European travel into Africa. The title of an article on Devex, the media platform for international development, asked: "Travel Restrictions Have Aid Workers Wondering: Is This Profession Viable Anymore?" (Lieberman 2020). If international travel is no longer simple and easily accessible, does it make sense to fly foreign people in to local offices? If meetings on Zoom become the norm, can technicians of poverty management do their jobs from the Washington or London or Geneva office and not claim the expat packages, visas, home leave, and hazard pay?

Even prior to the COVID pandemic, environmental factors had begun to put the restructuring of aid more frequently up for debate. The tremendous ecological footprint of the aid industry is still only rarely discussed, but it could become increasingly questioned as climate change continues to dominate headlines and logistics meetings. Organizations working to stem the myriad disastrous impacts of environmental change might find the optics of flying staff around the world for trainings and short-term missions more and more troubling.

The importance of localization has been discussed for decades, under various names, as far back as the OECD's 1996 *Shaping the 21st Century* report,[5] the World Bank's 1999 Comprehensive Development Framework,[6] and the UN's Millennium Challenge Goals Agenda. Nevertheless, despite its prominence as a key objective in global frameworks of development, localization remains largely elusive. Management and technical roles in development remain largely occupied by foreign expatriates. The reasons have more to do with development's history and foundation than with a lack of other alternatives.

For these reasons, critical development scholars advocate for not only a "local turn" but a decolonization of development. Decolonization starts from an understanding that the contemporary aid industry is rooted in the framework of European imperial conquest. Whereas localization advocates for a handover of the reins to local actors, decolonization interrogates the very apparatus changing hands. "Decoloniality asks: where do we start the story? Who has the microphone and who usually doesn't? What do we consider expertise? What are the implications of Eurocentric bias in knowledge production? Do our practices and knowledge systems contribute to the struggle against colonial power relations?" (Rutazibwa 2019, 66). A local turn in international development alone cannot achieve the goal of challenging the very foundations and structures of the industry.

To call for a decolonization of development confirms the connective tissue between colonialism and present-day development. To what extent is it fair to draw parallels from the colonial to contemporary development? Certainly, many of the aid workers I spent time with and interviewed would be horrified and offended or at the very least, annoyed by such parallels and their "unsettling consequences" (Stoler 2010, xviii), but how can one ignore such a significant part of the foundational origin of development discourses? As Fred Cooper (2002, 16) reminds us, even for post-independence African governments, development, in its most top-down constructions, was a continuation of most of the principles of colonial era projects.[7] The continuities between the colonial era and the present push us to think of these two periods as not wholly separate; as Uma Kothari puts it, "The trajectory from colonialism to development is more usefully characterized as a shift in emphasis" (2009, 161). "Coloniality" continues to shape global dynamics of power and their consequences, and this has clear expression in the contemporary development industry.[8]

Ann Stoler (2013) has referred to the lasting imperial processes, structures, and philosophies that live just under the surface of contemporary life in postcolonial places as "imperial debris." These remains "continue to organize social life and experience, underpinning present-day inequality and injustice" (Wright, Rolston, and Aoláin 2022, 2). To what extent can we conceive of contemporary practices of expatriate aid workers and their lifestyles in Senegal as a part of this imperial debris? Debris, in Stoler's conception, contains an aspect of rot and ruination, as the corrosive effects of empire are still terrifyingly alive, active and insidious in the postcolonial present. Within the development industry, the same "hierarchy of humanity" (Fassin 2010, 239) that upheld, legitimated, and excused imperial conquest in foreign lands still permeates the development project both in its logics and its everyday practice.[9] The well-compensated Western expats living in the same neighborhoods of a West African capital once inhabited by colonial migrants, employing local people in their homes to perform the same kinds of caring labor, and using the same territory as a place from which to make their careers and class identity can't help but embody within the development industry the "resonances and echoes" (Duffield and Hewitt 2009, 14) of the will to power and assumptions of entitlement that shaped imperial intervention.[10]

In this study, I have explored the relations between expat aid workers in postcolonial Africa and their local domestic workers to highlight the broader racialized and gendered dynamics of power that remain entrenched on the continent. The mismatched rewards that the development industry brings to its Western practitioners versus its target beneficiaries is a key point of emphasis. The demonstrated daily and long-term impact of a rotating door of expats posted to developing countries impels us to reflect on the development industry "as an industry," as Thomas W. Dichter has put it, "as having its own imperatives, as having its own survival at stake, more, increasingly, than the survival of its putative raison d'être—the poor people of the underdeveloped nations" (2003, 4).

The last time Fiona and I spoke, she and her husband were headed back to Europe. Their time in Dakar was done and they had new jobs awaiting them. She was worried for her children, who'd grown attached to the three people who looked after them—the housekeeper, the nanny, and the driver/childminder. "That'll be a big wrench for us when we leave," she said. She predicted their departure would be difficult for her house staff as well. "For them there's a big hole in their lives, on numerous levels, but fundamentally on a financial level, so I'm already seeing how I can—dare I say—put them to good homes? That expression!" She laughed at her own phrasing but continued, emphasizing her desire and her duty to see her staff placed in her idea of a good home. "It's important to me if I found someone who didn't think like we did and appreciate them and work with them as we did, then I would recommend that they work with another family. Because they work hard, they invest hard, you know, and I have a sense of responsibility." She quickly clarified, "While I'm here. When we go, it's a different life. Life moves on, and we go on to the next job."

In a parallel to many development projects themselves, once the intended time period of an expat's stint in Senegal is over, their domestic employees are left in a position not very different from that in which they were before. The employers have used the extracted care to reproduce and maintain their class status and prestige, to advance in their careers, and often to ensure the upward mobility of their children. The domestic workers, on the other hand, have found some temporary support and financial gain, but little that is sustainable and rarely transformative.

Notes

Introduction: Aid Work and the Extraction of Care

1. Names of all domestic workers and expat employers have been changed to protect their privacy.

2. One notable exception is Christian and Namaganda 2018.

3. Cf. Chin 2003; Lutz 2011; Lutz 2017.

4. Bigon and Hart (2018) point out that the urban grid of Dakar is not simply a top-down colonial innovation, but an interactive engagement between European urban design and the existing Lebou traditions of settlement, thus another illustration of Dakar's long history as a cosmopolitan melting pot of ideas.

5. See also Mbembe 2007.

6. See Beeckmans 2017, 366.

7. "Une population de passage," as Paul Mercier (1955, 134) put it. His study revealed that in the 1950s, less than half the population of Europeans in Dakar had been in West Africa for more than three years, and those who had, had resided in many different locations across the French West African Federation. No one he interviewed intended to remain definitively in West Africa; most planned to retire at home in Europe, where some had homes or apartments waiting (135).

8. As the city is on a peninsula and has only one direction for geographic expansion, efforts such as relocating the city's airport outside the city have been made to extend economic activity and residence to towns like Diamniadio, Rufisque, and Sebikotane. The aid industry is also primed to follow this trend, with the UN's plans to move its headquarters to Diamniadio in the coming years and other NGOs expected to follow suit.

9. See International Center for Not-for-Profit Law (ICNL) 2021.

10. See Michael (2004, 91–111) for an overview of the NGO landscape in Senegal.

11. My records reveal I made a total $1,850 in my first six months on the job, something the cash-strapped NGO justified by calling the high-pressure sixty-hour-a-week job an "internship."

12. See, for example, Mosse 2005; Cookson 2018, 127.

13. See also Gardner and Lewis 2015.

14. See Autesserre 2014, 175; McWha-Hermann 2011, 30.

15. *Whiteness* here does not imply that all expat development workers are white. Indeed, many are not and there are efforts to diversify the racial makeup of the staff of development organizations, though the majority of development expats are still white or coded white. Rather, *whiteness* here is understood as "a configuration of power, privilege and identity consisting of white racialized ideologies and practices, with material and social ramifications" (van Zyl-Hermann and Boersema 2017, 652) and "an everyday mechanism of privilege" (Hendriks 2017, 684).

16. See Harrison (2020) for how these designations are also rooted in industrial capitalism.

17. Escobar 1999; Rahnema and Bawtree 1997; Esteva 1992; Kothari 2006.

18. Cf. Moyo 2009.

19. Cf. Ferguson 1994; Jones 2013.

20. See Peters 2020; Cook-Lundgren 2022. This is also true of other globalized industries, including resource extraction. Pierre 2020; Appel 2019.

21. See Crewe and Harrison 1998 for a similar critique.

22. Peters 2020; Pascucci 2019; Fassin 2010; Ong and Combinido 2017; Roth 2015; Carr et al. 2010. See Michael (2004) for a related discussion of inequities among local vs. international NGOs.

23. See Crewe and Fernando 2006, 45.

24. See Cook-Lundgren 2022.

25. See Crewe and Fernando 2006, 51; see also Redfield 2012.

26. Carr et al. 2010; Dichter 2016; Carr, Chipande, and MacLachlan 1998.

27. See Kothari 2006 for more on these blind spots.

28. See also Smirl 2015, 208.

29. See Hannaford 2020.

30. See Moyo 2009; Easterly 2006; and many others for this critique.

31. Murphy 2015; Ticktin 2011; Coe 2019, 245–46.

32. See Paris (2002) on how peacebuilding efforts also echo the *mission civilatrice*.

33. Ferguson 1994; Murray Li 2007.

34. Escobar 1999; Gupta 1998.

35. Tsing 1993; Karim 2008.

36. Mosse 2011; Hindman and Fechter 2011; Shutt 2012; Nouvet and Jakinow 2016; Roth 2015.

37. A growing literature on this very topic has emerged in the last ten years, however. Cf. the research of Sarah Kunz (2016, 2020).

38. An easy case can be made for viewing colonial administrators as economic migrants as well, as Mercier's (1955, 1963) and Cruise O'Brien's (1972) studies illustrate.

39. Nowicka 2006; Loquercio, Hammersley, and Emmens 2006; Hunt 2011.

Chapter 1: Finding Help in the Informal Economy

1. The International Labour Organization (2015, 2016) and UN Women (2013) have also published studies on domestic worker conditions and treatment.

2. See Lan (2003) for how employers of domestic workers use food as a means to enact boundaries of social separation between themselves and their domestics. See also Coe (2019, 33–40) for a long discussion on food and relations between domestic workers and employers.

3. In another perfect illustration of the "small world" of the aid bubble, it turned out that I had stayed with these aid worker friends of Gemma's in the south of Senegal about ten years prior to this interview while returning to Dakar from a bike trip in the foothills of the Fouta Djallon, and I likely met her housekeeper then.

4. All names have been changed and contact information has been redacted.

5. The RSO is the embassy's Regional Security Officer. To say that this gardener is RSO-vetted is to say that the embassy has performed a background check and determined that he is a safe person to have on the property.

6. This is, in fact, why the American ambassador hired me to watch her pets despite having a full staff of domestic workers: she wanted to be sure her pets would be loved and cuddled in her absence, something she didn't expect from her housekeeper, whom she knew was not fond of animals.

7. Presumably, the advertiser means recipes with less oil, less spice, and fewer "funky" ingredients like *ketcha*, a dried, smoked fish.

8. Cf. Hochschild 2003.

9. Sea Plaza is a European-style mall on Dakar's coastal road, the Corniche.

10. See also Pilon et al. 2019, 137.

11. Chort, Vreyer, and Zuber 2020, 297; Brockerhoff and Eu 1993; Hamer 1981.

12. See Benoist (2008, 471) for more information on the various social programs of les Soeurs du Bon Pasteur in Dakar over the past forty years.

13. The center is named after the "little flower," also known as the "martyr to chastity," one of the youngest Catholic saints, an Italian girl who was canonized after dying rather than be sexually assaulted at age eleven. See Claassen-Lüttner 2013.

14. See Faty (2014) on the long and fascinating history of the convergence of language, religion, and politics in Senegal.

15. See Kantrowitz (2018) on how Catholic schooling shaped an elite class in post-colonial Senegal.

16. See Sow (2003) and Augis (2009) on women and veiling in Senegal; and Ba (2012) on conservative sects in Senegal.

17. Ndari 2018, 41; though see Diome (2013, 4) for even lower estimates from the National Confederation of Senegalese Workers.

18. Some domestic workers prefer this arrangement because it provides housing in Dakar, which can be costly for rural migrants who may not have ideal living arrangements in the city. This was also true for rural migrant domestic workers in colonial Dakar. Petrocelli 2020, 331.

19. See Burnham and Theodore 2012; Lair, MacLeod, and Budgar 2016.

20. See Ndari 2018, 14.

21. See Bop 2010; Diome 2013, 66.

22. See Boris and Klein 2014.

23. See also Lair, MacLeod, and Budgar 2016, 288; Hondagneu-Sotelo 2001, 120.

24. This rule only applies to official Foreign Service employees. Contractors and certainly host country national staff have no such obligation, though nearly all these people also employ domestic workers.

25. The lack of savings is widespread among domestic workers. See Coe (2019) on how African migrants who work in paid caring labor in the US find themselves equally unable to provide for a secure retirement through their work. Many must move home when they age out of their work.

Chapter 2: Security and Everyday Bordering

1. See Smirl 2015; Duffield 2012.

2. See also Roth 2015, 142.

3. See Duffield 2010.

4. Similarly, Hudson and Inkson (2006) talk about the "hero's adventure" approach to volunteering in the developing world.

5. Beeckmans 2017; Bigon 2016; Nelson 2007. See also Séquin (2021) on how even brothels in colonial Dakar played a role in enforcing a color bar.

6. Bigon, 2016, 92; Betts 1971. The four "communes" of Dakar, Saint Louis, Rufisque, and Gorée were unique spaces in French West Africa where the Senegalese residents, the *originaires*, were given first voting rights in 1848 and eventually full rights of French citizenship by the end of WWI.

7. Exceptions are separatist violence in the southern region of Casamance and a political riot in February 2021 that was treated by local and international observers as entirely out of step with Senegal's peaceful history.

8. US Department of State, *Country Reports on Terrorism 2017—Senegal*, 19 September 2018, https://www.refworld.org/docid/5bcf1f8413.html. This builds on a long history of extensive police surveillance in Senegal that began in the interwar colonial era. Keller 2012.

9. No such attack took place, and this same hotel was in 2017 the site of a high-profile terrorism simulation and training exercise by the Senegalese government.

10. A few who worked for the US government expressed mild anxiety in the wake of the 2016 presidential election about what the security ramifications of a Trump foreign policy would be for American citizens overseas.

11. See also Duffield 2012, 486.

12. This negative reputation was emblematized by a video that circulated on the internet in the spring of 2020. The video zoomed into a white UN SUV with the logo prominently displayed, traveling on a trafficked road, in which a UN employee could be seen in the back seat, straddled by a woman in a short red dress, presumably a sex worker, apparently having intercourse en route. After the video sparked an outcry, two UN employees were suspended for failing to observe the standards of conduct expected of international civil servants.

13. Surprisingly, it is USAID and not the French government that is the largest, most active, and arguably most respected donor to Senegal. See Michael 2004, 103, for possible explanations for this strong relationship.

14. Reputation was also key to domestic workers' employability in Dakar in the colonial era, as they faced increased competition as the city grew. So important was reputation at this time that some domestic workers went to colonial courts to have official records of how and why they had been wrongfully dismissed. Petrocelli 2020, 331–32.

15. See also the prevalence of such anecdotes in advertisements recommending domestic employees in the previous chapter.

Chapter 3: Stratigraphies of Mobility

1. Notable exceptions include Kunz 2016, 2020; Leonard 2010; and Fechter 2016.

2. See also Hannoum 2019.

3. See also van Rooij and Margaryan (2019) on the overlooked "unproblematic" intra-EU migration in public discourse on migration in Europe, or Ngwenya 2010 on the understudied African expat communities in Africa.

4. See Kunz (2016) for a more comprehensive literature review of scholarship on the topic of expatriates.

5. Van Bochove and Engbersen (2013) use this article to challenge both of these characterizations, arguing instead that expats do not make one distinctive group; however, their study is about largely white expats in Holland, which is markedly different from the questions of expats in Africa.

6. See Korpela 2019; D'Andrea 2016; Orel 2020; Woldorf and Litchfield 2021.

7. See Warnes 2009; Botterill 2011; Oliver 2008; Bender, Hollstein, and Schweppe 2018; Berman 2017.

8. See Hannaford (2021) on Dakar's unique amenities for expats.

9. Cole (2016, 124) notes that this enhanced status also allows European expats in Africa more access to marriage with locals.

10. Leonard (2010) rightly points out that this increased status is contingent for many expats, as class differences between executives and lower-status positions lead to different opportunities for advancement and long-term financial stability.

11. See Cruise O'Brien (1972, 27) on how members of the French community also remained in Senegal in the first decade post-independence to "profit from the inflated expatriate salaries which would eventually provide for a better life in France."

12. Cruise O'Brien (1972, 60) even finds Senegalese complaints during the colonial period about trailing spouses that mirror today's concerns, "the wives of civil servants" filling jobs in the colonial administration that could have gone to local people.

13. See also Cruise O'Brien 1972, 82.

14. A few fathers interviewed echoed this as well.

15. *Fatou* has another meaning in France, where it is generally used as a derogatory term for a lower-class West African young woman.

16. Domestic workers for expats, however, very commonly are from the southern Casamance region, as I note in chapter 1.

17. Bop 2010; Diop 2010.

18. Lambert 2002; Linares 2003; Guigou and Lericollais 1992.

19. Diop and Diouf 1990; Ndiaye 2009.

20. See Cruise O'Brien 1971; Diop 1981; Diouf 2000; Ebin 1992; Riccio 2004; Hannaford 2017.

21. Creevey, Vengroff, and Gaye 1995, 674; Saffari 2013, 43.

22. See Bujra 1983, 122.

23. See Nader 2015. These dynamics are similar elsewhere in the region as well. Cf. Jacquemin 2009; Human Rights Watch 2007.

24. Gassama 2005, 171. See also chapter 1.

25. The Lebanese community has been an economic and social fixture in Dakar for generations, and thus they are not considered Senegalese but are not considered expats. See Leichtman 2015.

26. Modou Diome 2013 gives a particularly descriptive assessment of the living conditions of most rural-urban migrant domestic workers: "The precarious shelters, the slums and the unfinished houses where they squat, their overcrowded rooms that they rent as a group, give witness, in part, to their itinerant situation and their poverty" (67; my translation).

27. Coe 2014 unpacks how wages in most sectors where international migrants work are insufficient to support a family in the host country, leading to "scattered families" (4).

28. Domestic workers I spoke to were vaguely aware of opportunities to do domestic work abroad, but not as clearly as were the Ghanaian care workers of Cati Coe's 2021 study, who had real expectations that their experience as care workers in Ghana could lead to lucrative caring gigs overseas (183).

29. Cf. Hondagneu-Sotelo and Avila 1997; Parreñas 2005; Gamburd 2000; Asis 2006.

30. See Gasparetti and Hannaford 2009; Coe 2014, 63.

31. See more on how this culture of migration shapes intimate life in Hannaford 2017.

32. Literally, "white-people projects," a colloquial reference to international development programs.

33. For just a few examples, cf. Hondagneu-Sotelo 2001; Lan 2006; Lutz 2016; Parreñas 2001b and 2005; Yeates 2009.

34. Notable exceptions are Wang 2013; and Lundström 2013.

35. See Christian and Namaganda 2018, 317.

36. See also Lundström (2013) for similar consequences where both employer and domestic employee are migrants.

37. See Jokela (2018) for more on the patterns of precarity in domestic work overall.

38. Hondagneu-Sotelo 2001; Parreñas 2015.

Chapter 4: Inequalities of the World Personified

1. See Wo 2019.

2. An example widely shared among aid workers at the time was a short-lived Kenyan television show called *The Samaritans*, created in 2014 about the office life of a fictional NGO in Nairobi called Aid for Aid. The show, shot mockumentary style with a madcap energy that was a mix of *Veep* and *The Office*, parodied the familiar archetypes who work in development, their petty grievances and power plays, and the wasteful uselessness of their work.

3. The "Secret Aid Worker" column on the *Guardian*'s website published a post that captured many of the same ambivalences: https://www.theguardian.com/global-development-professionals-network/2015/dec/29/secret-aid-worker-how-can-we-fight-inequality-if-we-live-as-privileged-expats.

4. *Farang* is a Thai word for foreigner/white person; *mzungu* is a Swahili word for the same thing. The equivalent in Senegal would be *toubab*.

5. See de Jong 2011.

6. Manji 1998; Ferguson 1994; Barnett 2012.It is also the grounding philosophy of much of philanthro-capitalism in general. Giridharadas 2019; Papazoglakis 2018.

7. Duffield and Hewitt 2009; Kothari 2009; Conklin 1997.

8. Mendez (1998) shows that domestic workers also use the strategy of "strategic personalism" to curry favor with employers and extract flexibility or support.

9. See, for example, the statement on the film by the Association of Black Women Historians: https://abwh.org/2011/08/12/an-open-statement-to-the-fans-of-the-help/.

10. Carly is referring a squat toilet, a toilet that has no basin but is a ceramic hole in the ground that flushes.

11. See Fountain (2011, 101) for parallels among expat aid workers in Indonesia.

12. See Lan (2003) on how food management is often part of boundary making among domestic employers and their employees.

13. However, Parreñas (2001b) convincingly illustrates how domestic workers can strategically utilize this fictive kinship to their advantage as well.

14. See also Rollins 1985.

15. As Ann Stoler (2010, 196) found in her interviews with former domestic servants of colonial families in Indonesia, a "good" boss was a bland and thin descriptor, which could mean anything from simply that they paid in full and on time to they occasionally said "please" before a command; "'good' in no way muted the gestures of subordination built into colonial relations."

16. These kinds of sponsorship programs have drawn no small amount of criticism for their paternalism and reproduction of colonial-era relations of power and knowledge. See Nolan 2020.

17. See Crewe and Harrison (1998) for more examples of development discourses that frame local people as morally or culturally unfit to manage their own affairs.

18. Wang (2013, 12) similarly found that many expat women living in Hong Kong sought to minimize their discomfort with their lavish lifestyles through volunteering for charitable causes.

19. Cf. Oloruntoba 2020; Moyo 2009.

Conclusion

1. The transnational aspects of this instance of the global care chain may also impede solidarity. Cruise O'Brien (1972) found that expat French people in Dakar in the 1960s who had once held radical leftist, even socialist politics in Europe came to live like petit bourgeoisie in Dakar, drawing on their racial and citizenship privilege to live above their earlier station. She gives as an example that they had "'boys' to do domestic work" (102). She also found that the expats' politics became more conservative and less solidarity-minded as a result of their upward mobility.

2. See Razavi and Miller 1995.

3. Like many neoliberal development initiatives, these well-meaning "gender and development" programs have received criticism for their real outcomes for "targeted beneficiaries." Cf. Karim 2008; Elias 2013; Boyd 2016; Moore 2016; Wilson 2015.

4. The "local turn" has been more closely debated in peacebuilding and conflict studies. See MacGinty and Richmond 2013; Van Leeuwen et al. 2020; Lundqvist and Öjendal 2018.

5. Available at https://www.oecd.org/dac/2508761.pdf.

6. Available at https://documents1.worldbank.org/curated/en/ 208631583185352783/pdf/The-comprehensive-development-framework .pdf.

7. See also Renders 2002, 61.

8. See Cook-Lundgren (2022) for a clear discussion of coloniality and how it shapes relations of power within NGOs.

9. Among others, Ziai (2013) argues that this is a good reason to scrap the entire concept of development.

10. See Watson (2013) for how this coloniality is embodied by aid workers.

Bibliography

Africa, Caribbean and Pacific Observatory on Migration (ACP). (2012). "La migration des filles mineures en Afrique de l'Ouest: Le cas du Sénégal." *Dossier d'information* D105. Brussels: ACP. https://publica tions.iom.int/books/la-migration-des-filles-mineures-en-afrique-de -louest-le-cas-du-senegal.

Alvarez Tinajero, S. P. (2014). *Migration Management? Accounts of Agricultural and Domestic Migrant Workers in Ragusa (Sicily)*. Genève: Graduate Institute Publications.

Anderson, Bridget. (2000). *Doing the Dirty Work: The Global Politics of Domestic Labor*. London: Zed Books.

Appel, Hannah. (2019). *The Licit Life of Capitalism: US Oil in Equatorial Guinea*. Durham, NC: Duke University Press.

Apthorpe, R. (2005). "Postcards from Aidland, Or: Love from Bubbleland." Paper presented at a graduate seminar at IDS, University of Sussex, 10 June.

Asis, M. M. B. (2006). "Living With Migration." *Asian Population Studies* 2, no. 1: 45–67.

Augis, Erin. (2009). "Les jeunes femmes sunnites et la libéralisation économique à Dakar." *Afrique contemporaine* 3, no. 231: 77–97.

Autesserre, Séverine. (2014). *Peaceland: Conflict Resolution and the Everyday Politics of International Intervention*. New York: Cambridge University Press.

Ba, Mame-Penda. (2012). "La diversité du fondamentalisme sénégalais." *Cahiers d'études africaines* 52, no. 206–7: 575–602.

Barnett, Allyson (2011). "Determinants of Internal Remittances: A Study of Migrant Domestic Workers Living in Dakar, Senegal." Honors thesis, University of Pittsburgh.

Barnett, M. (2012). "International Paternalism and Humanitarian Governance." *Global Constitutionalism* 1, no. 3: 485–521.

Basse, Arona. (2011). "Initiative de la CNTS de former des travailleuses domestiques: Une idée généreuse d'aider ces femmes à se prendre en charge." *Le Quotidien*. https://www.lequotidien.sn/lequotidienarch ives/index.php/component/k2/item/25953-initiative-de-la-cnts-de -former-des-travailleuses-domestiques-une-idée-généreuse-d'aider -ces-femmes-à-se-prendre-en-charge.

Beck, Erin. (2017). *How Development Projects Persist: Everyday Negotiations with Guatemalan NGOs*. Durham, NC: Duke University Press.

Beeckmans, Luce. (2017). "The 'Development Syndrome': Building and Contesting the SICAP Housing Schemes in French Dakar (1951–1960)." *Canadian Journal of African Studies / Revue canadienne des études africaines* 51, no. 3: 359–88.

Bender, Désirée, Tina Hollstein, and Cornelia Schweppe. (2018). "International Retirement Migration Revisited: From Amenity Seeking to Precarity Migration?" *Transnational Social Review* 8, no. 1: 98–102.

Benoist, Joseph-Roger de. (2008). *Histoire de l'Église catholique au Sénégal: Du milieu du XVe siècle à l'aube du troisième millénaire*. Paris: Kathala.

Berman, Nina. (2017). *Germans on the Kenyan Coast: Land, Charity, and Romance*. Indianapolis: Indiana University Press.

Bernstein, Elizabeth. (2007). *Temporarily Yours: Intimacy, Authenticity, and the Commerce of Sex*. Chicago: University of Chicago Press.

Betts, Raymond F. (1971). "The Establishment of the Medina in Dakar, Senegal, 1914," *Africa* 41, no. 2: 143–52.

Bianchi, S. M. (2011). "Changing Families, Changing Workplaces." *The Future of Children* 21, no. 2: 15–36.

Bigon, Liora. (2016). *French Colonial Dakar: The Morphogenesis of an African Regional Capital*. Manchester: Manchester University Press.

Bigon, Liora, and Thomas Hart. (2018). "Beneath the City's Grid: Vernacular and (Post-) Colonial Planning Interactions in Dakar, Senegal." *Journal of Historical Geography* 59: 52–67.

Blum, Jon. (2020). "Localization in the COVID-19 Era." *InterAction*, 21 August. https://www.interaction.org/blog/localization-in-the-covid -19-era/.

Bonacker, T., J. von Heusinger, and K. Zimmer, eds. (2019). *Localization in Development Aid: How Global Institutions Enter Local Lifeworlds*. Abingdon: Routledge.

Bop, Codou. (2010). "Femme, migration et protection sociale: Cas des migrations internes et transfrontalières fillettes au Sénégal et du Mali." Symposium du CODESRIA sur le genre 2010, *Genre, migration et développement socio-économique en Afrique*, Cairo, 24–26 November 2010.

Boris, E., and J. Klein. (2014). "The Fate of Care Worker Unionism and the Promise of Domestic Worker Organizing: An Update." *Feminist Studies* 40, no. 2: 473–79.

Boris, E., and R. S. Parreñas. (2010). *Intimate Labors: Cultures, Technologies, and the Politics of Care*. Stanford, CA: Stanford University Press.

Borneman, John. (2017). "Afterword: Further Questions about the Global Care Chain." *Ethics and Social Welfare* 11, no. 3: 296–303.

Bornstein, Erica. (2012). *Disquieting Gifts: Humanitarianism in New Delhi*. Stanford, CA: Stanford University Press.

Botterill, Kate. (2011). "Discordant Lifestyle Mobilities in East Asia: Privilege and Precarity of British Retirement in Thailand." *Population, Space and Place* 23: 1–11.

Brockerhoff, M., and Hongsook Eu. (1993). "Demographic and Socioeconomic Determinants of Female Rural to Urban Migration in Sub-Saharan Africa." *International Migration Review* 27, no. 3 (September): 557–77.

Bruno-van Vijfeijken, Tosca. (2019). "'Culture Is What You See When Compliance Is Not in the Room': Organizational Culture as an Explanatory Factor in Analyzing Recent INGO Scandals." *Nonprofit Policy Forum* 10, no. 4.

Bujra, Janet M. (1983). "Class, Gender and Capitalist Transformation in Africa." *Africa Development* 8, no. 3: 17–42.

Burnham, L., and Theodore, N. (2012). *Home Economics: The Invisible and Unregulated World of Domestic Work*. New York: National Domestic Workers Alliance.

Carr, Stuart C., T. Rose Chipande, and Malcolm MacLachlan. (1998). "Expatriate Aid Salaries in Malawi: A Doubly Demotivating Influence." *International Journal of Educational Development* 18, no. 2: 133–34.

Carr, Stuart C., I. McWha, M. MacLachlan, and A. Furnham. (2010). "International–Local Remuneration Differences across Six Countries: Do They Undermine Poverty Reduction Work?" *International Journal of Psychology* 45, no. 5: 321–40.

Carter, Donald M. (1997). *States of Grace: Senegalese in Italy and the New European Immigration*. Minneapolis: University of Minnesota Press.

Chin, C. B. N. (2003). "Visible Bodies, Invisible Work: State Practices toward Migrant Women Domestic Workers in Malaysia." *Asian and Pacific Migration Journal* 12, no. 1–2: 49–73.

Chort, I., P. de Vreyer, and T. Zuber. (2020). "Mobilité genrée au Sénégal." *Population* 75, no. 2: 297–323.

Christian, Michelle, and Assumpta Namaganda. (2018). "Transnational Intersectionality and Domestic Work: The Production of Ugandan Intersectional Racialized and Gendered Domestic Worker Regimes." *International Sociology* 33, no. 3: 315–36.

Claassen-Lüttner, J. C. (2013). *Witnessing Maria Goretti: Testimonial Practices for a Silent Martyr*. PhD dissertation, Emory University.

Clarke, Gerard. (2021). "The Credibility of International Non-Governmental Organizations (INGOs) and the Oxfam Scandal of 2018." *Journal of Civil Society* 17, no. 3–4: 219–37.

Coe, Cati. (2014). *The Scattered Family: Parenting, African Migrants, and Global Inequality*. Chicago: University of Chicago Press.

———. (2019). *The New American Servitude: Political Belonging among African Immigrant Home Care Workers*. New York: New York University Press.

———. (2021). *Changes in Care: Aging, Migration, and Social Class in West Africa*. New Brunswick, NJ: Rutgers University Press.

Coggin, Ross. (1978). "The Development Set." *Journal of Communication* 28, no. 1: 80.

Cole, Jennifer. (2016). "Entangled Postcolonial Futures: Malagasy Marriage Migrants and Provincial Frenchmen." In *African Futures: Essays on Crisis, Emergence, and Possibility*, ed. Brian Goldestone and Juan Obarrio. Chicago: University of Chicago Press.

Conklin, Alice L. (1997). *A Mission to Civilize: The Republican Idea of Empire in France and West Africa, 1895–1930*. Stanford, CA: Stanford University Press.

Cook-Lundgren, Emily. (2022). "Theorizing the Persistence of Local-Foreign Inequality in International Development Organizations through the Analytic of Coloniality." *Gender, Work, and Organization*, 1 March. https://doi.org/10.1111/gwao.12826.

Cookson, Tara Patricia. (2018). *Unjust Conditions: Women's Work and the Hidden Cost of Cash Transfer Programs*. Berkeley: University of California Press.

Cooper, F. (2002). *Africa since 1940: The Past of the Present*. Cambridge: Cambridge University Press.

Cooper, Glenda. (2021). "#AidToo: Social Media Spaces and the Transformation of the Reporting of Aid Scandals in 2018." *Journalism Practice* 15, no. 6: 747–66.

Coquery-Vidrovitch, Catherine. (1993). "La ville africaine: 'Lieu de colonisation.'" *Afrique Contemporaine* 168: 11–22.

Cranston, S. 2017. "Expatriate as a 'Good' Migrant: Thinking through Skilled International Migrant Categories." *Population, Space and Place* 23: e2058.

Creevey, Lucy, R. Vengroff, and I. Gaye. (1995). "Devaluation of the CFA Franc in Senegal: The Reaction of Small Businesses." *Journal of Modern African Studies* 33, no. 4: 669–83.

Crewe, Emma, and Priyanthi Fernando. (2006). "The Elephant in the Room: Racism in Representations, Relationships and Rituals." *Progress in Development Studies* 6, no. 1: 40–54.

Crewe, Emma, and Elizabeth Harrison. (1998). *Whose Development? An Ethnography of Aid*. London: Zed Books.

Cruise O'Brien, Donal B. (1971). *The Mourides of Senegal: The Political and Economic Organization of an Islamic Brotherhood*. Oxford: Clarendon.

Cruise O'Brien, Rita. (1972). *White Society in Black Africa: The French of Senegal*. Evanston, IL: Northwestern University Press.

D'Andrea, A. (2016) "Neo-nomadism: A Theory of Post-identitarian Mobility in the Global Age." *Mobilities* 1, no. 1: 95–119.

David, N. (2010). "Spotlight Interview with Fatou Bintou Yaffa (CNTS-Senegal)." International Trade Union Confederation. 1 January. https://www.ituc-csi.org/spotlight-interview-with-fatou.

de Jong, Sara. (2011). "False Binaries Altruism and Selfishness in NGO Work." In *Inside the Everyday Lives of Development Workers: The Challenges and Futures of Aidland*, ed. A. Fechter and H. Hindman, 21–40. New York: Kumarian.

de la Bellacasa, M. P. (2011). "Matters of Care in Technoscience: Assembling Neglected Things." *Social Studies of Science* 41, no. 1: 85–106.

Diaw, Bamba. (1996). "Participatory Research Is the First Step Towards Political Action: The Case of Young Female Domestic Servants in Dakar, Senegal." *Childhood* 3: 271–77.

Dichter, Thomas. (2003). *Despite Good Intentions: Why Development Assistance to the Third World Has Failed*. Amherst: University of Massachusetts Press.

———. (2016). "Why USAID's New Approach to Development Assistance Is Stalled: Speaking Out." *Foreign Service Journal*, December. https://www.afsa.org/why-usaids-new-approach-development-assistance-stalled.

Diome, Modou. (2013). "Les formes d'exploitation des 'bonnes à tout faire' en milieu urbain dakarois." In *Pratiques d'esclavage et d'asservissement des femmes en Afrique: Les cas du Sénégal et de la République Démocratique du Congo*, ed. Ndèye Sokhna Guèye. Dakar: CODESRIA.

Diop, M.-C. (1981). "Fonctions et activités des *Dahira* mourides urbaines" (Sénégal). *Cahiers d'Études Africaines* 21: 79–91.

Diop, M.-C., and Diouf, M. (1990). *Le Sénégal sous Abdou Diouf*. Paris: Karthala.

Diop, Rosalie Aduyai. (2010). *Survivre à la pauvreté et à l'exclusion: Le travail des adolescents dans les marchés de Dakar*. Paris: Afrima-Karthala-CREPOS.

Diouf, M. (2000). "The Senegalese Murid Trade Diaspora and the Making of a Vernacular Cosmopolitanism." *Public Culture* 12, no. 3: 679–702.

Drążkiewicz-Grodzicka, E. M. (2018). "Work in Crisis: Managing Fantasies about Distant Strangers, Managing Aid Workers." *Social & Cultural Geography* 6: 812–30.

Drotbohm, Heike. (2015). "Shifting Care among Families, Social Networks, and State Institutions in Times of Crisis: A Transnational Cape Verdean Perspective." In *Anthropological Perspectives on Care: Work, Kinship and the Life-Course*, ed. Erdmute Alber and Heike Drotbohm, 93–116. New York: Palgrave Macmillan.

D'Souza, A. (2010). *Le travail domestique sur la voie du travail décent: Réunion d'experts sur le status et les conditions d'emploi des gens de maison.* Geneva: ILO.

Duffield, Mark. (2010). "Risk-Management and the Fortified Aid Compound: Everyday Life in Post-Interventionary Society." *Journal of Intervention and Statebuilding* 4, no. 4: 453–74.

———. (2012). "Challenging Environments: Danger, Resilience and the Aid Industry." *Security Dialogue* 43, no. 5: 475–92.

Duffield, Mark, and Vernon Hewitt, eds. 2009. *Empire, Development and Colonialism: The Past in the Present.* Rochester, NY: Boydell & Brewer.

Duffy, Mignon. 2007. "Doing the Dirty Work: Gender, Race, and Reproductive Labor in Historical Perspective." *Gender & Society* 21: 313–36.

Duffy, Mignon, Amy Armenia, and Clare L. Stacey. (2015). *Caring on the Clock: The Complexities and Contradictions of Paid Care Work.* New Brunswick, NJ: Rutgers University Press.

Easterly, William. (2006). *The White Man's Burden: Why the West's Efforts to Aid the Rest Have Done So Much Ill and So Little Good.* New York: Penguin Press.

Ebin, V. (1992). "À la recherche de nouveaux 'poissons': Stratégies commerciales mourides par temps de crise." *Politique Africaine* 45: 86–99.

Egeland, J., A. Harmer, and A. Stoddard. (2011). *To Stay and Deliver: Good Practice for Humanitarians in Complex Security Environments.* New York: Policy Development and Studies Bureau, UN Office for the Coordination of Humanitarian Affairs.

Elias, Juanita. (2013). "Davos Women to the Rescue of Global Capitalism: Postfeminist Politics and Competitiveness Promotion at the World Economic Forum." *International Political Sociology* 7, no. 2: 152–69.

Escobar, Arturo. (1999). "The Invention of Development." *Current History* 98, no. 631: 382–86.

Esteva, G. (1992). "Development." In *The Development Dictionary, a Guide to Knowledge as Power*, ed. W. Sachs, 6–25. London: Zed Books.

Faeth, P. C., and M. G. Kittler. (2017). "How Do You Fear?" *Journal of Global Mobility: The Home of Expatriate Management Research* 5, no. 4: 391–417.

Fall, François Seck, Luis Orozco, and Al-Mouksit Akim. (2020). "Adoption and Use of Mobile Banking by Low-Income Individuals in Senegal." *Review of Development Economics* 24: 569–88.

Fanon, Frantz. 1963. *The Wretched of the Earth*. Preface by Jean-Paul Sartre. Translated by Constance Farrington. New York: Grove Press.

Faria, C. (2020). "Call for Papers." *ACME: An International Journal for Critical Geographies* 19, no. 2: 413–23.

Fassin, Didier. (2010). "Inequality of Lives, Hierarchies of Humanity: Moral Commitments and Ethical Dilemmas of Humanitarianism." In *In the Name of Humanity: The Government of Threat and Care*, ed. Ilana Feldman and Miriam Ticktin, 238–255. Durham, NC: Duke University Press.

———. (2011). "Noli Me Tangere: The Moral Untouchability of Humanitarianism." In *Forces of Compassion : Humanitarianism Between Ethics and Politics*, ed. Erica Bornstein and Peter Redfield. Santa Fe, NM: School for Advanced Research Press.

Faty, El Hadj Abdul Aziz. (2014). "Politiques linguistiques au Sénégal au lendemain de l'Indépendance: Entre idéologie et realisme politique." *Mots: Les langages du politique* 106: 13–26.

Fechter, A.-M. (2011). "'Anybody at Home?' The Inhabitants of Aidland." In *Inside the Everyday Lives of Development Workers: The Challenges and Futures of Aidland*, ed. A. Fechter and H. Hindman, 131–50. New York: Kumarian.

———. (2012). "'Living Well' while 'Doing Good'? (Missing) Debates on Altruism and Professionalism in Aid Work." *Third World Quarterly* 33, no. 8: 1475–91.

———. (2016). "Aid Work as Moral Labour." *Critique of Anthropology* 36, no.3: 228–43.

Ferguson, James. (1994). *The Anti-Politics Machine: Development, Depoliticization, and Bureaucratic Power in Lesotho*. Minneapolis: University of Minnesota Press.

Foreign Service Institute (FSI). (2016). *Foreign Service Assignment Notebook*. Arlington, VA: US Department of State, FSI, Transition Center.

Foucher, Vincent. (2005). "Relationships between Men and Women and the Building of a Casamençais Identity." *Cahiers d'Études Africaines* 178, no. 2: 431–55.

Fountain, P. (2011). "Orienting Guesthood in the Mennonite Central Committee, Indonesia." In *Inside the Everyday Lives of Development Workers : The Challenges and Futures of Aidland*, ed. H. Hindman and A.-M. Fechter. Sterling, VA: Kumarian Press.

Fredericks, Rosalind. (2018). *Garbage Citizenship: Vital Infrastructure of Labor in Dakar, Senegal*. Durham, NC: Duke University Press.

Gamburd, M. R. (2000). *The Kitchen Spoon's Handle: Transnationalism and Sri Lanka's Migrant Households*. Ithaca, NY: Cornell University Press.

Gardner, Katy, and David Lewis. (2015). *Anthropology and Development: Challenges for the Twenty-First Century*. London: Pluto Press.

Gasparetti, Fedora, and Dinah Hannaford. (2009). "Genitorialità a distanza: reciprocità e migrazione senegalese." *Mondi Migranti* 1: 111–31.

Gassama, Absa. (2005). "Les marchés du travail domestique au Sénégal." *Innovations* 2, no. 22: 171–84.

Geertz, Clifford. (1982). "The Way We Think Now: Toward an Ethnography of Modern Thought." *Bulletin of the American Academy of Arts and Sciences* 35, no. 5: 14–34.

Ging-Dawan Boyd, Ginger. (2016). "The Girl Effect: A Neoliberal Instrumentalization of Gender Equality." *Consilience: The Journal of Sustainable Development* 15, no. 1: 146–80.

Giridharadas, Anand. (2019). *Winners Take All: The Elite Charade of Changing the World*. First Vintage Books ed. New York: Vintage.

Glenn, Evelyn Nakano. (1986). *Issei, Nisei, War Bride: Three Generations of Japanese American Women in Domestic Service*. Philadelphia: Temple University Press.

———. (1992). "From Servitude to Service Work: Historical Continuities in the Racial Division of Paid Reproductive Labor." *Signs* 18, no. 1: 1–43.

———. (2012). *Forced to Care: Coercion and Caregiving in America*. Cambridge, MA: Harvard University Press.

Gorer, Geoffrey. (1935). *Africa Dances: A Book about West African Negroes*. New York: Alfred A. Knopf.

Guigou, Brigitte, and André Lericollais. (1992). "Crise de l'agriculture et marginalization économique des femmes sereer siin (Sénégal)." *Sociétés—Espaces—Temps* 1: 45–64.

Gupta, A. (1998) *Postcolonial Developments: Agriculture in the Making of Modern India*. Durham, NC: Duke University Press.

Hamer, Alice. (1981). "Diola Women and Migration: A Case Study." In *The Uprooted of the Western Sahel: Migrants' Quest for Cash in the Senegambia*, ed. L. G. Colvin et al., 183–203. New York: Prager.

Hancock, G. (1989). *Lords of Poverty: The Power, Prestige, and Corruption of the International Aid Business*. New York: Atlantic Monthly Press.

Hannaford, Dinah. (2017). *Marriage without Borders: Transnational Spouses in Neoliberal Senegal*. Philadelphia: University of Pennsylvania Press.

———. (2020). "Having It All Overseas: Aid Workers and the International Division of Reproductive Labor." *Gender, Work and Organization* 27: 565–80.

———. (2021). "Human Infrastructure in Expat Spaces of an African City." *City and Society* 33, no. 2: 279–412.

Hannoum, A. (2019). *Living Tangier: Migration, Race, and Illegality in a Moroccan City*. Philadelphia: University of Pennsylvania Press.

Harmer, A., A. Stoddard, and V. Di Domenico. (2011). "Aiding Education in Conflict: The Role of International Education Providers Operating in Afghanistan and Pakistan." *Prospects* 41: 205–11.

Harrison, Elizabeth. (2013). "Beyond the Looking Glass? 'Aidland' Reconsidered." *Critique of Anthropology* 33, no. 3: 263–79.

Harrison, Graham. (2020). *Developmentalism: The Normative and Transformative within Capitalism*. Oxford, UK: Oxford University Press.

Heathershaw, John. (2016). "Who Are the 'International Community'? Development Professionals and Liminal Subjectivity." *Journal of Intervention and Statebuilding* 10, no. 1:77–96.

Hendriks, T. (2017). "A Darker Shade of White: Expat Self-Making in a Congolese Rainforest Enclave." *Africa* 87 (4): 683–701.

Hesseling, Gerti. (1985). *Histoire politique du Sénégal: Institutions, droit et société*. Paris: Ed. Karthala.

Hindman, H., and Fechter, A.-M. (2011). *Inside the Everyday Lives of Development Workers: The Challenges and Futures of Aidland*. Sterling, VA: Kumarian Press

Hochschild, Arlie. (2003). "Love and Gold." In *Global Woman: Nannies, Maids and Sex Workers in the New Economy*, ed. Arlie Hochschild and Barbara Ehrenreich. New York: Metropolitan Press.

Hom, Sabrina. (2007). "Housekeepers and Nannies in the Homework Economy: On the Morality and Politics of Paid Housework." In *Global Feminist Ethics: Feminist Ethics and Social Theory*, ed. Peggy Desautels and Rebecca Whisnant, 23–41. Lanham, MD: Rowman & Littlefield.

Hondagneu-Sotelo, Pierrette. (2001). *Doméstica: Immigrant Workers Cleaning and Caring in the Shadows of Affluence*. Berkeley: University of California Press.

———. (2007). "Blowups and Other Unhappy Endings." In *Domestica: Immigrant Workers Cleaning and Caring in the Shadows of Affluence*, 114–34. With new preface. Berkeley: University of California Press.

Hondagneu-Sotelo, Pierrette, and Ernestine Avila. (1997). "'I'm Here, But I'm There': The Meanings of Latina Transnational Motherhood." *Gender and Society* 11: 548–71.

Hudson, S., and K. Inkson. (2006). "Volunteer Overseas Development Workers: The Hero's Adventure and Personal Transformation." *Career Development International* 11, no. 4: 304–20.

Human Rights Watch. (2007). *Au bas de l'échelle: Exploitation et maltraitance des filles travaillant comme domestiques en Guinée*. Human Rights Watch report, 15 juin. https://www.hrw.org/fr/report/2007/06/15/au-bas-de-lechelle/exploitation-et-maltraitance-des-filles-travaillant-comme

Humanitarian Women's Network. (2016). *Humanitarian Women's Network Full Survey Results*. https://interagencystandingcommittee.org/system/files/hwn_full_survey_results_may_2016.pdf.

Hunt, Matthew. (2011). "Establishing Moral Bearings: Ethics and Expatriate Health Care Professionals in Humanitarian Work." *Disasters* 35, no. 3: 606–22.

Hutter, M. (2014). "'My Filipina Is from Ghana': Transnational Migration, Nannies, and Family Life." *Journal of Comparative Family Studies* 44, no. 6: 741–48.

International Center for Not-for-Profit Law (ICNL). (2021). *Senegal.* https://www.icnl.org/resources/civic-freedom-monitor/senegal.

International Federation of Red Cross and Red Crescent Societies (IFRC). (2011). *Stay Safe: The International Federation's Guide for Security Managers.* 20 June. https://reliefweb.int/report/world/stay-safe-inter national-federation's-guide-security-managers.

International Labour Organization. (2015). *ILO Global Estimates on Migrant Workers: Research and Methodology.* Geneva: Switzerland.

———. (2016). *Worker, Helper, Auntie, Maid?: Working Conditions and Attitudes Experienced by Migrant Domestic Workers in Thailand and Malaysia.* Geneva: International Labour Organization.

Jacquemin, M. (2009). "'Petites nièces' et 'petites bonnes' à Abidjan: Les mutations de la domesticité juvenile." *Travail, genre et sociétés* 2, no. 22: 53–74.

Jokela, Merita. (2018). *Patterns of Precarious Employment in a Female-Dominated Sector in Five Affluent Countries: The Case of Paid Domestic Labor Sector in Five Welfare States.* LIS Working Paper Series, no. 746. Luxembourg: Luxembourg Income Study.

Jones, Branwen G. (2013). "'Good Governance' and 'State Failure': Genealogies of Imperial Discourse." *Cambridge Review of International Affairs* 26, no. 1: 49–70.

Kantrowitz, R. (2018). "Catholic Schools as 'a Nation in Miniature': Catholic Civism in Senegal and Benin, 1960–1970s." *Journal of African History* 59, no. 2: 221–39.

Karim, L. (2008). "Demystifying Micro-credit: The Grameen Bank, NGOs, and Neoliberalism in Bangladesh." *Cultural Dynamics* 20, no. 1: 5–29.

Keller, Kathleen A. (2012). "Political Surveillance and Colonial Urban Rule: 'Suspicious' Politics and Urban Space in Dakar, Senegal, 1918–1939." *French Historical Studies* 35, no. 4: 727–49.

Kibora, L. O. (2019). "Réactions populaires aux attaques terroristes de janvier 2016 à Ouagadougou." *Mande Studies* 21: 55–69.

Korpela, Mari. (2020). "Searching for a Countercultural Life Abroad: Neo-nomadism, Lifestyle Mobility or Bohemian Lifestyle Migration?" *Journal of Ethnic and Migration Studies* 46, no. 15: 3352–69.

Kothari, Uma. (2006). "Critiquing 'Race' and Racism in Development Discourse and Practice." *Progress in Development Studies* 6, no. 1: 1–7

———. (2009). "Spatial Practices and Imaginaries: Experiences of Colonial Officers and Development Professionals." In *Empire, Development and Colonialism: The Past in the Present.* ed. M. Duffield and V. Hewitt, 161–75. Rochester, NY: Boydell & Brewer.

Kunz, Sarah. (2016). "Privileged Mobilities: Locating the Expatriate in Migration Scholarship." *Geography Compass* 10, no. 3: 89–101.

———. (2020). "Expatriate, Migrant? The Social Life of Migration Categories and the Polyvalent Mobility of Race." *Journal of Ethnic and Migration Studies* 46, no. 11: 2145–62.

Lair, C., C. MacLeod, and E. Budgar. (2016). "Advertising Unreasonable Expectations: Nanny Ads on Craigslist." *Sociological Spectrum* 36, no. 5: 286–302.

Lambert, Michael. (2002). *Longing for Exile: Migration and the Making of a Translocal Community in Senegal.* Portsmouth, NH: Heinemann.

Lan, Pei-Chia. (2003). "Negotiating Social Boundaries and Private Zones: The Micropolitics of Employing Migrant Domestic Workers." *Social Problems* 50, no. 4: 525–49.

———. (2006). *Global Cinderellas: Migrant Domestics and Newly Rich Employers in Taiwan.* Durham, NC: Duke University Press.

Lee, Sabine, and Susan Bartels. (2020). "'They Put a Few Coins in Your Hand to Drop a Baby in You': A Study of Peacekeeper-fathered Children in Haiti." *International Peacekeeping* 27, no. 2: 177–209.

Leichtman, Mara A. (2015). *Shi'i Cosmopolitanisms in Africa: Lebanese Migration and Religious Conversion in Senegal.* Indianapolis: Indiana University Press.

Leonard, P. (2010). *Expatriate Identities in Postcolonial Organizations: Working Whiteness.* Farnham, UK: Ashgate Publishing.

Lieberman, Amy. (2020). "Travel Restrictions Have Aid Workers Wondering: Is This Profession Viable Anymore?" News. Devex. https://www.devex.com/news/travel-restrictions-have-aid-workers-wondering-is-this-profession-viable-anymore-97861.

Linares, Olga F. (2003). "Going to the City . . . and Coming Back? Turnaround Migration among the Jola of Senegal." *Africa* 73, no. 1: 113–32.

Loquercio, D., M. Hammersley, and B. Emmens. (2006). *Understanding and Addressing Staff Turnover in Humanitarian Agencies.* Humanitarian Practice Network Paper 55. London: Overseas Development Institute. http://www.odihpn.org/documents/networkpaper055.pdf.

Lundqvist, M. O., and J. Öjendal. (2018). "Atomised and Subordinated? Unpacking the Role of International Involvement in 'The Local Turn' of Peacebuilding in Nepal and Cambodia." *Journal of Peacebuilding & Development* 13, no. 2: 16–30.

Lundström, Catrin. (2013). " 'Mistresses' and 'Maids' in Transnational 'Contact Zones': Expatriate Wives and the Intersection of Difference and Intimacy in Swedish Domestic Spaces in Singapore." *Women's Studies International Forum* 36: 44–53.

Lutz, Helma. (2011). *The New Maids: Transnational Women and the Care Economy*. London: Zed Books.

———, ed. (2016.) *Migration and Domestic Work: A European Perspective on a Global Theme*. London: Routledge.

———. (2017). "Care as a Fictitious Commodity: Reflections on the Intersections of Migration, Gender and Care Regimes." *Migration Studies* 5, no. 3: 356–68.

MacGinty, Roger, and Olivier P. Richmond, (2013). "The Local Turn in Peace Building: a Critical Agenda for Peace." *Third World Quarterly* 34, no. 5: 763–83.

Madore, Frédérik. (2016). "The New Vitality of Salafism in Côte d'Ivoire: Toward a Radicalization of Ivoirian Islam?" *Journal of Religion in Africa* 46, no. 4: 417–52.

Manji, Firoze. (1998). "The Depoliticisation of Poverty." In *Development and Rights*, ed. D. Eade, 12–33. Development in Practice Reader. Oxford: Oxfam GB.

Manji, Firoze, and Carl O'Coill. (2002). "The Missionary Position: NGOs and Development in Africa." *International Affairs* 78, no. 3: 567–83.

M'Baye, Babacar. (2019). "Afropolitan Sexual and Gender Identities in Colonial Senegal." *Humanities* 8, no. 4: 166.

Mbembe, Achille. (2007). "Afropolitanism." In *Africa Remix: Contemporary Art of a Continent*, ed. Njami Simon and Lucy Durán, 26–29. Johannesburg: Johannesburg Art Gallery.

McIlwaine, C., and Bunge, D. (2019). "Onward Precarity, Mobility and Migration among Latin Americans in London." *Antipode: A Radical Journal of Geography* 51, no. 2: 601–19.

McWha-Hermann, Ishbel. (2011). "The Roles of, and Relationships between, Expatriates, Volunteers, and Local Development Workers." *Development in Practice* 21: 29–40.

Melly, C. (2010). "Inside-out Houses: Urban Belonging and Imagined Futures in Dakar, Senegal." *Comparative Studies in Society and History* 52, no. 1: 37–65.

Mendez, J. (1998). "Of Mops and Maids: Contradictions and Continuities in Bureaucratized Domestic Work." *Social Problems* 45, no. 1: 114–35.

Mercier, Paul. (1955). "Le groupement européen de Dakar: Orientation d'une enquête." *Cahiers Internationaux de Sociologie* 19: 130–46. http://www.jstor.org/stable/40688931.

———. (1965). "Evolution of Senegalese Elites." In *Africa: Social Problems of Change and Conflict*, ed. Pierre L. Van den Berghe, 163–78. San Francisco: Chandler Publishing.

Michael, Sarah. (2004). *Undermining Development: The Absence of Power among Local NGOs in Africa*. Oxford: Oxford University Press.

Moore, Erin. (2016). "Postures of Empowerment: Cultivating Aspirant Feminism in a Ugandan NGO." *Ethos* 44, no. 3: 375–96.

Mosse, D. (2005). *Cultivating Development: An Ethnography of Aid Policy and Practice*. London and Ann Arbor, MI: Pluto Press.

———, ed. (2011). *Adventures in Aidland. The Anthropology of Professionals in International Development*. New York: Berghahn Books.

Mottola, Matthew, and Matthew Coatney. (2021). *The Human Cloud: How Today's Changemakers Use Artificial Intelligence and the Freelance Economy to Transform Work*. New York: Harper Collins.

Moyo, Dambisa. (2009). *Dead Aid: Why Aid Is Not Working and How There Is a Better Way for Africa*. New York: Farrar, Straus and Giroux.

Murphy, Michelle. (2015). "Unsettling Care: Troubling Transnational Itineraries of Care in Feminist Health Practices." *Social Studies of Science* 45, no. 5: 717–37.

Murray Li, Tania. (2007). *The Will to Improve: Governmentality, Development, and the Practice of Politics*. Durham, NC: Duke University Press.

Nader, Antara S. (2015). *Maid for Success: Locating Domestic Work in Senegal's Shifting Landscape of Gender, Labor, and Power*. Anthropology Honors Projects, 25, DeWitt Wallace Library, Macalester College. https://digitalcommons.macalester.edu/anth_honors/25.

Nakamura, Shohei, Rawaa Harati, Somik V. Lall, Yuri M. Dikhanov, Nada Hamadeh, William Vigil Oliver, Marko Olavi Rissanen, and Mizuki Yamanaka. (2019). "Is Living in African Cities Expensive?" *Applied Economics Letters* 26, no. 12: 1007–12.

Ndari, Gebbe. (2018). *Santé sexuelle et reproductive des filles domestiques "FATOU" à Dakar*. Mauritius: Éditions Universitaires Européennes.

Ndiaye, Ndioro. (2009). "Migration and Small Urbanisation : The Case of Senegal." *Rural 21 : International Journal for Rural Development* 43, no. 2: 18–21.

Nelson, David. (2007). "Defining the Urban: The Construction of French-Dominated Colonial Dakar, 1857–1940." *Historical Reflections / Réflexions Historiques* 33, no. 2: 225–55.

Nguyen, Mihn T. N. (2014). "Fictitious Kinship: Intimacy, Relatedness and Boundaries in the Life of Hanoi's Migrant Domestic Workers." *Cambridge Journal of Anthropology* 32, no. 2: 81–96.

Ngwenya, Nomfundo. (2010). "African Expatriate Communities in Africa: Their Size, Lifestyles and Relationship with Their Sending State." *Africa Insight* 40, no. 1 (June). https://hdl.handle.net/10520/EJC17633.

Nolan, Kathleen. (2020). "Better Than Nothing? A Review and Critique of Child Sponsorship." *Research Society and Development* 9, no. 8: e26985574.

Nouvet, E., and Jakinow, T. (2016). "Moral Sentiments in Aidland: Aid and Development as Moral Experience." *Critique of Anthropology* 36. no. 3: 223–27.

Nowicka, M. (2006). *Transnational Professionals and Their Cosmopolitan Universes*. Frankfurt am Main; New York: Campus Verlag.

Oliver, C. (2008). *Retirement Migration: Paradoxes of Ageing*. London: Routledge.

Oloruntoba, Samuel Ojo. (2020). "The Politics of Paternalism and Implications of Global Governance on Africa: A Critique of the Sustainable Development Goals." In *Pan Africanism, Regional Integration and Development in Africa*, ed. Samuel Ojo Oloruntoba, 165–80. Cham, CH: Palgrave Macmillan.

Ong, Jonathan Corpus, and Combinido, Pamela. (2017). "Local Aid Workers in the Digital Humanitarian Project: Between 'Second Class Citizens' and 'Entrepreneurial Survivors.'" *Critical Asian Studies* 50, no. 1: 86–102.

Orel, M. (2020). "Life Is Better in Flip Flops: Digital Nomads and Their Transformational Travels to Thailand." *International Journal of Culture, Tourism and Hospitality Research* 15, no. 1: 3–9.

Ozyegin, Gul. (2001). *Untidy Gender: Domestic Service in Turkey.* Philadelphia: Temple University Press.

Pailey, Robtel Neajai. (2020). "De-centering the 'White Gaze' of Development." *Development and Change* 51, no. 3: 729–45.

———. (2021). "Race in/and Development." In *The Essential Guide to Critical Development Studies*, 2nd ed., ed. Henry Veltmeyer and Paul Bowles, 31–39. Abingdon, Oxon: Routledge.

Papazoglakis, Sarah. (2018). "Doing Good, Behaving Badly: Fictions of Philanthropy in the Americas." PhD diss., University of California Santa Cruz.

Paris, Roland. (2002). "International Peacebuilding and the 'Mission Civilisatrice." *Review of International Studies* 28: 637–56.

Parreñas, Rhacel Salazar. (2001a). "Mothering from a Distance: Emotions, Gender, and Intergenerational Relations in Filipina Transnational Families." *Feminist Studies* 27, no. 2: 361–90.

———. (2001b). *Servants of Globalization: Women, Migration and Domestic Work.* Stanford, CA: Stanford University Press.

———. (2005). *Children of Global Migration: Transnational Families and Gendered Woes.* Stanford, CA: Stanford University Press.

———. (2008). *The Force of Domesticity: Filipina Migrants and Globalization.* New York : New York University Press.

———. (2015). *Servants of Globalization: Migration and Domestic Work.* 2nd ed. Stanford, CA: Stanford University Press.

Parreñas, Rhacel Salazar, Krittiya Kantachote, and Rachel Silvey. (2020). "Soft Violence: Migrant Domestic Worker Precarity and the Management of Unfree Labour in Singapore." *Journal of Ethnic and Migration Studies* 47, no. 20: 4671–87.

Pascucci, E. (2019). "The Local Labour Building the International Community: Precarious Work within Humanitarian Spaces." *Environment and Planning A: Economy and Space* 51, no. 3: 743–60.

Peng, Ito. (2018). "Shaping and Reshaping of Care and Migration in East and Southeast Asia." *Critical Sociology* 44, no. 7–8: 1117–32.

Perry, D. L. (1997). "Rural Ideologies and Urban Imaginings: Wolof Immigrants in New York City." *Africa Today* 44, no. 2: 229–59.

Peters, Rebecca Warne. (2020). *Implementing Inequality: The Invisible Labor of International Development.* New Brunswick, NJ: Rutgers University Press.

Petrocelli, Rachel M. (2020). "Reputations at Stake: Positioning Self and Others in Dakar's Colonial Court, 1922–1942." *International Journal of African Historical Studies* 53, no. 3: 315–33.

Pierre, Jemima. (2012). *The Predicament of Blackness: Postcolonial Ghana and the Politics of Race.* Chicago: University of Chicago Press.

———. (2013) "Race in Africa Today: A Commentary." *Cultural Anthropology* 28, no. 3: 547–51.

———. (2020). "The Racial Vernaculars of Development: A View from West Africa." *American Anthropologist* 122, no.1: 86–98.

Pilon, Marc, Valérie Delaunay, Richard Marcoux, Aminata Coulibaly, and Binta Dieme. (2019). "Essai de mesure et d'analyse de la présence de domestiques dans les ménages en Afrique subsaharienne." *Politique africaine* 2, no. 154: 121–43.

Rahnema, Majid, and Victoria Bawtree. (1997). *The Post-Development Reader.* London: Zed Books.

Rajak, D., and Stirrat, J. (2011). "Parochial Cosmopolitanism and the Power of Nostalgia." In *Adventures in Aidland: The Anthropology of Expertise and Professionals in Development* ed. D. Mosse. New York: Berghahn Books.

Razavi, S., C. Miller, and World Conference on Women. (1995). *From WID to GAD: Conceptual Shifts in the Women and Development Discourse.* Geneva: United Nations Research Institute for Social Development.

Redfield, Peter. (2012). "The Unbearable Lightness of Ex-Pats: Double Binds of Humanitarian Mobility." *Cultural Anthropology* 27, no. 2: 358–82.

Renders, Marleen. (2002). "An Ambiguous Adventure: Muslim Organizations and the Discourse of 'Development' in Senegal." *Journal of Religion in Africa* 32, no. 1: 61–82.

Riccio, B. (2004). "Transnational Mouridism and the Afro-Muslim Critique of Italy." *Journal of Ethnic and Migration Studies* 30, no. 5: 929–44.

Rollins, Judith. (1985). *Between Women: Domestics and their Employers.* Philadelphia: Temple University Press.

Roth, S. (2015). "Aid Work as Edgework—Voluntary Risk-Taking and Security in Humanitarian Assistance, Development and Human Rights Work." *Journal of Risk Research* 18, no. 2: 139–55.

Rutazibwa, Olivia Umurerwa. (2019). "What's There to Mourn? Decolonial Reflections on (the End of) Liberal Humanitarianism." *Journal of Humanitarian Affairs* 1, no. 1: 65–67.

Saffari, Siavash. (2013). "Alternative Development(s), or Alternative(s) to Development?: Challenges and Prospects for Genuine Alternative-Building." In *Africa Yesterday, Today & Tomorrow: Exploring the Multi-dimensional Discourses on 'Development,'* ed. Nathan N. Andrews, Ernest Khalema, Temitope Oriola, and Isaac Odoom, 40–51. Newcastle, UK: Cambridge Scholars Publishing.

Séquin, Caroline. (2021). "Marie Piquemal, the "Colonial Madam": Brothel Prostitution, Migration, and the Making of Whiteness in Interwar Dakar." *Journal of Women's History* 33, no. 4: 118–41.

Shutt, C. (2012). "A Moral Economy? Social Interpretations of Money in Aidland." *Third World Quarterly* 33, no. 8: 1527–43.

Silvey, Rachel, and Rhacel Parreñas. (2020). "Precarity Chains: Cycles of Domestic Worker Migration from Southeast Asia to the Middle East." *Journal of Ethnic and Migration Studies* 46, no. 16: 3457–71.

Slim, H. (1995). "What Is Development?" *Development in Practice* 5, no. 2: 143–48.

Smirl, Lisa. (2015). *Spaces of Aid: How Cars, Compounds, and Hotels Shape Humanitarianism.* London: Zed Books.

Sow, Fatou. (2003). "Fundamentalisms, Globalisation and Women's Human Rights in Senegal." *Gender and Development* 11, no. 1: 69–76

Standing, Guy. (2011). *The Precariat: The New Dangerous Class.* London: Bloomsbury Academic.

Stirrat, R. L. (2000). "Cultures of Consultancy." *Critique of Anthropology* 20, no. 1: 31–46.

Stoddard, A., A. Harmer, and V. DiDomenico. (2008). *The Use of Private Security Providers and Services in Humanitarian Operations.* Humanitarian Policy Group, report 27, October.

Stoler, Ann. (2010). *Carnal Knowledge and Imperial Power.* 2nd ed. Berkeley: University of California Press.

———. (2013). *Imperial Debris: On Ruins and Ruination.* Durham, NC: Duke University Press.

Ticktin, Miriam I. (2011). *Casualties of Care: Immigration and the Politics of Humanitarianism in France.* Berkeley: University of California Press.

Tronto, Joan. (1993). *Moral Boundaries: A Political Argument for an Ethic of Care*. New York: Routledge.

Trouillot, Michel-Rolph. (1991). "Anthropology and the Savage Slot: The Poetics and Politics of Otherness." In *Recapturing Anthropology: Working in the Present*, ed. Richard G. Fox, 17–44. New Brunswick, NJ: Rutgers University Press.

Tsing, A. (1993). *In the Realm of the Diamond Queen: Marginality in an Out-of-the-Way Place*. Princeton, NJ: Princeton University Press.

Understanding Children's Work (UCW). (2010). *Comprendre le travail des enfants et l'emploi des jeunes au Senegal: Rapport du pays*. Rome: UCW, February. https://www.researchgate.net/publication/279849434_Comprendre_le_travail_des_enfants_et_l%27emploi_des_jeunes_au_Senegal.

UN Women. (2013). *Domestic Workers Count Too: Implementing Protection for Domestic Workers*. Briefing kit. New York: United Nations Entity for Gender Equality and the Empowerment of Women (UN Women). https://www.unwomen.org/sites/default/files/Headquarters/Attachments/Sections/Library/Publications/2013/3/UNWomen_IUTC_Factsheets%20pdf.pdf.

van Bochove, M., and Engbersen, G. (2013). "Beyond Cosmopolitanism and Expat Bubbles: Challenging Dominant Representations of Knowledge Workers and Trailing Spouses." *Population, Space and Place* 21: 295–309.

Vance, C. M., Y. McNulty, Y. Paik, and J. D'Mello. (2016). "The Expatpreneur: Conceptualizing a Growing International Career Phenomenon." *Journal of Global Mobility* 4, no. 2: 202–24.

Van Leeuwen, Mathijs, Joseph Nindorera, Jean-Louis Kambale Nzweve, and Corita Corbijn. (2020). "The 'Local Turn' and Notions of Conflict and Peacebuilding—Reflections on Local Peace Committees in Burundi and Eastern DR Congo." *Peacebuilding* 8, no. 3: 279–99.

van Rooij, Niek, and Lusine Margaryan. (2019). "Integration of 'Ideal Migrants': Dutch Lifestyle Expat-preneurs in Swedish Campgrounds." *Rural Society* 28, no. 3: 183–97.

van Zyl-Hermann, Danelle, and Jacob Boersema. (2017). "Introduction: The Politics of Whiteness in Africa." *Africa* 87, no. 4: 651–61.

Verma, Ritu. (2011). "Intercultural Encounters, Colonial Continuities, and

Contemporary Disconnects in Rural Aid: An Ethnography of Development Practitioners in Madagascar." In *Inside the Everyday Lives of Development Workers : The Challenges and Futures of Aidland*, ed. H. Hindman and A.-M. Fechter. Sterling, VA: Kumarian Press.

Wang, Leslie. (2013). "Unequal Logics of Care: Gender, Globalization and Volunteer Work of Expatriate Wives in China." *Gender & Society* 27, no. 2: 538–60.

Warnes, T. (2009). "International Retirement Migration." In *International Handbook of Population: Aging*, ed. P. Uhlenberg. International Handbooks of Population, vol 1. Dordrecht: Springer.

Watson, Marcus D. (2013). "The Colonial Gesture of Development: The Interpersonal as a Promising Site for Rethinking Aid to Africa." *Africa Today* 59, no. 3: 3–28.

White, Sarah. (2002). "Thinking Race, Thinking Development." *Third World Quarterly* 23, no. 3: 407–19.

Wilson, Kalpana. (2015). "Towards a Radical Re-appropriation: Gender, Development and Neoliberal Feminism." *Development and Change* 46, no. 4: 803–32.

Wo, Lai Y. (2019). "Intimate Economy of Vulnerability: Transactional Relationships between Western Expatriates and Southeast Asian Domestic Workers in Hong Kong's Wanchai." *Research in Economic Anthropology* 38: 153–74.

Woldorf, Rachael A., and Robert C. Litchfield. (2021). *Digital Nomads: In Search of Freedom, Community, and Meaningful Work in the New Economy*. New York: Oxford University Press.

Wright, Claire, Bill Rolston, and Fionnuala Ní Aoláin. (2022). "Navigating Colonial Debris: Structural Challenges for Colombia's Peace Accord." *Peacebuilding*, 24 January. doi: 10.1080/21647259.2022.2027153.

Yeates, N. (2009). "Production for Export: The Role of the State in the Development and Operation of Global Care Chains." *Population, Space and Place* 15: 175–87.

Yeoh, Brenda S. A., and Shirlena Huang. (2010). "Transnational Domestic Workers and the Negotiation of Mobility and Work Practices in Singapore's Home-Spaces." *Mobilities* 5, no. 2: 219–36.

Young, C. (1994). *African Colonial State in Comparative Perspective*. New Haven, CT: Yale University Press.

Yuval-Davis, Nira, Georgie Wemyss, and Kathryn Cassidy. (2018). "Everyday Bordering, Belonging and the Reorientation of British Immigration Legislation." *Sociology* 52, no. 2: 228–44.

Ziai, Aram. (2013) ."The Discourse of 'Development' and Why the Concept Should Be Abandoned." *Development in Practice* 23, no. 1: 123–36.

Index

Abidjan, Ivory Coast, 74
abuse, 29, 30, 56, 57, 62, 65
accusations, 59, 96, 97, 142. *See also*
    treatment of domestic workers
ACLU, 64
advertisements, 26, 31, 36, 141,
    164n7; expats consult, 1, 32;
    expats create for employees, 63;
    for female-gendered workers,
    41; for gardener, 39; include
    cooking repertoire, 43; include
    job-specific qualities, 37; include
    male employee's emotional
    connection, 40; include personal
    qualities, 46; include reasonable
    salary requirement, 51; include
    specific tasks, 45; include work
    dedication, 42; for nannies, 44;
    by Senegalese employers, 56; on
    social media, 22
advocacy, 64, 65, 158

Afghanistan, 68, 70, 73
Africa, 110, 149; affordable domestic
    care in, 98; aid workers in, 3, 18;
    colonial settings in, 5; Dakar's
    differences from, 71; Europeans
    in, 157, 167n9; expats in, 2, 100,
    105, 166n3, 167n5, 167n9; fishbowl
    syndrome in, 76; food more ex-
    pensive in, 113; governments of,
    158; humanitarian good works
    of empire in, 20; migration in,
    110, 120; postcolonial, 102, 122,
    159; US passport in, 24; Western
    migration to, 155
Africans, 4, 24, 71, 72, 119, 166n3;
    cast as helpless children, 150;
    migrants, 165n25
Afropolitanism, colonial, 4
agencies, 23, 73, 123; aid/development,
    5–6, 16, 17, 23, 70, 107, 147–48;
    behavior of, 88; employment, 31;

GLOBALIZATION
IN EVERYDAY LIFE

As global forces undeniably continue to change the politics and economies of the world, we need a more nuanced understanding of what these changes mean in our daily lives. Significant theories and studies have broadened and deepened our knowledge on globalization, yet we need to think about how these macro processes manifest on the ground and how they are maintained through daily actions.

Globalization in Everyday Life foregrounds ethnographic examination of daily life to address issues that will bring tangibility to previously abstract assertions about the global order. Moving beyond mere illustrations of global trends, books in this series underscore mutually constitutive processes of the local and global by finding unique and informative ways to bridge macro- and microanalyses. This series is a high-profile outlet for books that offer accessible readership, innovative approaches, instructive models, and analytic insights to our understanding of globalization.
